Book"marks"

Please feel free to initial or make a special "mark" in the square to keep track of books you've read.

"Polio is a horrible disease, and Thuhang's story underscores the challenges of surviving it. I appreciate her tenacious spirit and uplifting message."

—BILL GATES

"*Standing Up After Saigon* is an engaging, authentic, well-written story that is both personal and significant for providing geopolitical context from the perspective of a Vietnamese family. This is a rare resource for readers interested in a story of resilience and personal courage and for readers who want to understand more about this era in Vietnam and America's shared history."

—CLAUDIA KENNEDY
First female three-star general in the US Army,
retired in 2000 after thirty-one years of military service;
author, *Generally Speaking*

"In today's world, filled with so many challenges—be it personal, cultural, environmental, or political—we all need stories of perseverance, unification, and family. This is a book of hope for peace, using our daily struggles to make us stronger. You realize at our core we must continue to believe in something that is bigger than who we are and beyond our current difficult environment. This is a story of all the above and one that inspires the soul to continue to strive and dream beyond today's circumstance. Embrace the diversity of life, the meaning of hope, and the light that continues to burn in each of us as you turn the pages."

—ROLLIN FORD
Retired EVP and CAO, Walmart

"Sharon Orlopp and Thuhang Tran have written what will soon be an international classic. *Standing Up After Saigon* is about the triumph of the human spirit and the power of one woman's determination and leadership to thrive. Read it."

—NELL MERLINO
Creator, Take Our Daughters to Work Day; author, activist, speaker, and consultant focused on empowering girls and women

"Sharon Orlopp has beautifully written Thuhang Tran's story. Sharon has accurately captured the history of this brave, tenacious little lady and what Vietnamese families went through after the fall of Saigon. My respect for the South Vietnamese is even greater after reading *Standing Up After Saigon*. This is a one-of-a-kind book. Every veteran, as well as all of America, will want to hug Thuhang and say, 'Way to go, sweetheart—we love you.'"

—BOB FORD
Author, *Black Cat 2-1*; Vietnam helicopter pilot;
CEO, Okeene Milling Company

"Fascinating story of survival and achievement with an outstanding demonstration of love, determination, and personal reinvention. A must-read."

—DR. MOHAMMAD BHUIYAN
Professor of entrepreneurship, Tuskegee University;
former US Congressional candidate

"Thuhang Tran's firsthand account of daily life in Vietnam once Saigon fell is extraordinary. She faced ongoing challenges of polio, poverty, famine, Communist economic programs, and family separation with grit, perseverance, and hope. Her riveting odyssey demonstrates the universal lesson of personal triumph despite unrelenting odds."

—**BERNIE MILANO**
President, KPMG Foundation;
creator, PhD Project, a nonprofit organization

"An invaluable sociological resource that recounts what life was like under the Viet Cong. This storied life in book form encourages us to continually seek new perspectives and expand our understanding—especially when it seems we are faced with insurmountable odds. Both a solemn reminder and inspiring account of humanity and perseverance, Thuhang's story reminds us of our innate human ability to dream, hope, and do whatever it takes to flourish."

—**KEVIN TURNER**
Retired COO, Microsoft

"*Standing Up After Saigon* enforces in us the powerful lessons of perseverance. Tran's riveting personal story of strength and courage to overcome life's insurmountable obstacles reminds us that the immigrant perspective fuels one's human capacity to see opportunities others don't, do what others won't, and keep pushing when prudence says quit."

—**GLENN LLOPIS**
Founder, Center for Hispanic Leadership,
and author of *The Innovation Mentality*

"The book is a riveting depiction of the struggles and hardships experienced by many immigrants as they navigate rigid immigration policies, while also exposing the realities of being a person with a disability in the developing world. Sharon Orlopp does a phenomenal job of telling a compassionate story of overcoming the odds despite tragedy that leaves us with a sense of optimism in knowing that with the love and support of family, anything is possible."

—ROHINI ANAND
Chief diversity officer, Sodexo, and board member
of the National Organization on Disability

"This book will captivate—and humble—anyone whose parents or grandparents suffered to reach this country and realize its promise. Few had it tougher than Thuhang, who spent her childhood crawling on her stomach due to crippling polio. She survives to make it from war-ravaged Vietnam to start a new life in America. The story of Thuhang's struggles and ultimate triumph helps us understand how America's immigrant heritage made it the greatest country on Earth and why it is so wrong to disdain and malign those immigrants of today who wish to help make our country even greater."

—JOSE VILLARREAL
Senior advisor and partner of Akin Gump; chairman of US Mexico
Foundation; political strategist and immigration reform advocate

STANDING UP AFTER SAIGON

STANDING UP AFTER SAIGON

The Triumphant Story of Hope, Determination, and Reinvention

Thuhang Tran

with

Sharon Orlopp

BROWN BOOKS
PUBLISHING GROUP

Standing Up After Saigon
The Triumphant Story of Hope, Determination, and Reinvention

Brown Books Publishing Group
16250 Knoll Trail Drive, Suite 205
Dallas, Texas 75248
www.BrownBooks.com
(972) 381-0009

A New Era in Publishing®

Publisher's Cataloging-In-Publication Data

Names: Tran, Thuhang, 1970- | Orlopp, Sharon.
Title: Standing up after Saigon : the triumphant story of hope, determination, and reinvention / Thuhang Tran, with Sharon Orlopp.
Description: Dallas, Texas : Brown Books Publishing Group, [2018]
Identifiers: ISBN 9781612549897
Subjects: LCSH: Tran, Thuhang, 1970- | Vietnam War, 1961-1975--Personal narratives, Vietnamese. | Poliomyelitis--Patients--Vietnam--Biography. | Women with disabilities--Vietnam--Biography. | Vietnamese American women--Biography. | LCGFT: Autobiographies. | Personal narratives.
Classification: LCC DS559.5 .T73 2018 | DDC 959.7043092--dc23

ISBN 978-1-61254-989-7
LCCN 2017958653

Printed in the United States
10 9 8 7 6 5 4 3 2 1

For more information or to contact the authors, please go to
www.StandingUpAfterSaigon.com

To my mom, Lieu Thi Pham,
for her unconditional love and dedication.

To my dad, Chinh Van Tran,
for being my constant and inspirational role model.

To both of my parents for their love and sacrifices.

TABLE OF CONTENTS

PART III: THUHANG

PART IV: CHINH

PREFACE

This book is not intended to be a history of South Vietnam or the Vietnam War. This is my own personal history based on facts, memory, and creative license. This is my story as I remember it. Dates, scenes, locations, and conversations are based on my recall, as well as on conversations with others about the events. Some names and other identifying details have been changed.

The term Viet Cong means Vietnamese Communist. I use the overall term Viet Cong rather than differentiating between members of the National Liberation Front and soldiers in the North Vietnamese Army. Diacritical marks that are part of the Vietnamese language are used in the poem I wrote, but for ease of reading, they are not used in the text of my story.

My memoir is my gift to you—particularly for those who feel invisible, underappreciated, underutilized, made fun of, disrespected, and not valued. Hope is the fuel that made the difference and kept me alive. Unwavering determination kept me focused on my future and enabled me to continually reinvent myself due to constantly changing circumstances. Personal reinventions during my moments of darkest despair provided powerful new beginnings.

I hope that my journey as a person who is an immigrant and differently abled will build bridges of interconnectedness and cultural understanding and give inspiration to treating all people with dignity, respect, and inclusion.

—Thuhang Tran

INTRODUCTION

Life is serendipitous. One of my friends, Hua Wang, suggested via text that I should meet with a Vietnamese woman, Thuhang Tran, to hear her personal story. He did not provide many details about her journey. Several months later, while visiting Thuhang's city, I met her for a cup of coffee.

Thuhang is a petite woman whose infectious, positive energy captivated me immediately. I barely noticed she walked with crutches. After listening to her mesmerizing story, I was spellbound and said, "You need to write a book about your life journey."

Thuhang matter-of-factly replied, "I've been waiting to find the right person to help me share my story."

To which I quickly said, "I'll help you write your book."

Thuhang's poignant odyssey starts with an extraordinary eyewitness account of life in Saigon once South Vietnam was conquered by the Communists. There is very little written about life in Vietnam once the Vietnam War ended. Her story is a rare and revealing account of the daily battle against starvation, poverty, and ideological oppression.

Her story of survival against the odds is even more dramatic because she contracted polio as a toddler and became unable to walk and run. Thuhang crawled on the floor for seventeen years. Thuhang's father, Chinh, constantly researched polio treatments. At age five, Thuhang was scheduled to travel from Saigon to West Germany for a revolutionary new polio treatment. Her dreams of walking were painfully destroyed and deferred due to the fall of Saigon.

Chinh was an air traffic controller for the South Vietnam Air Force; he worked alongside Americans while stationed at Da Nang, Saigon, and Can Tho. He narrowly escaped to America when the war ended. His family was erroneously told that he had been killed in a helicopter crash. Thuhang's family held his funeral service and mourned his death for three years in Vietnamese tradition.

While Thuhang and her family struggled to stay alive with Communist-controlled economic programs and famine levels of food rationing, Chinh was challenged with starting a new life in America. His first job was as a short-order cook for minimum wage. He continually wrote letters to his family in Saigon to see if they were alive. What he didn't realize was that the new regime had changed the names of cities and streets; the numeric system of house addresses was also changed. His letters were never received by his family.

After five years of undeterred resilience, Chinh located his family through the help of friends. Due to strained relations and immigration battles between the United States and Vietnam, it took ten more years before the family was reunited. Chinh's unrelenting focus on finding his family and ensuring they would eventually be reunited after fifteen years of separation demonstrates the power of love.

The story doesn't end with family reunification. Thuhang's riveting firsthand account of being a differently abled immigrant illustrates the indomitable power of the human spirit and the potential that exists within each of us, regardless of how others may label, categorize, or minimize. Her unquenchable spirit of hope creates a tale of resilience that is more amazing than any fiction I have read.

Once Thuhang arrived in America, she had surgery that enabled her to walk with the aid of leg braces and crutches. She stood upright after crawling on the ground and viewing life at floor level for seventeen years. It is an emotionally stirring portrait of hope, sheer determination, and continual personal reinvention. Her unforgettable quest provides universal lessons about personal triumph in the face of dramatic adversity.

Thuhang's story immediately grabbed me and wouldn't let go. It's a story that needs to be told because it is a powerful reminder that against overwhelming odds, humans can prevail. Her journey is a gift of courage, hope, perseverance, and family love.

—Sharon Orlopp

Tưởng nhớ 31 năm

Tuổi Thơ Tôi Đâu?

———————————

Mới ngần ấy tuổi đầu, tôi biết
  khóc
  khóc,
tôi sợ nhìn những xác chết đầy
  đường
ngay giữa ban ngày, ngày lịch sử
  không quên

Mới ngần ấy tuổi đầu, tôi biết
  thương
thương Mẹ
mỗi ngày lấm lem bùn "kinh tế
  thủy lợi"

Mới ngần ấy tuổi đầu, tôi khát
  khao
ước làm người lớn
thay Mẹ rẫy rừng hoang - "kinh
  tế mới"

Và cũng tuổi thơ ấy, tôi xanh xao
gầy gộc với những củ khoai lang
  sùng cắt xén

Tuổi thơ tôi đó, ngày ngày ngồi tẻ
  bắp
giúp Mẹ đi đổi ít hạt gạo, bo bo

In Memory of Thirty-One
Years after Black April

Where Was My Childhood?

———————————

When I was young, I cried
Cried
Afraid of seeing dead bodies on
  the street
In daylight, the day of history
  unforgettable

As young as I was, I learned to
  love and
My heart ached when I saw Mom
Covered with dirt and mud head
  to toe, from the work they
  called "irrigation economy"

As young as I was, I wish
Wishing I could become an adult
  fast
To help Mom work on the farm,
  far away in the wild highlands,
  "subsidized economy" the name
  they called

Then my childhood endured
  sickness, pale thin to bones,
  result of lack of nutrition in
  rotten sweet potatoes

During my childhood, I detached
  corn pulp from the cobs
Helped Mom exchange corn for
  rice

Ngày tháng trôi, nước mắt tôi ráo hoảnh
vì khóc vùi nhớ Mẹ nhớ Cha

Cũng ngần ấy tuổi đầu, tôi biết sợ
sợ người đêm đêm
ghé xóm bắt anh tôi đi "thanh niên xung phong"
qua chiếm đất Lào

Để từ đó, tôi biết lo
phập phồng mỗi khi có tiếng chó sủa đầu ngõ
rồi xa dần . . . bớt lo, biết rằng anh tôi chưa bị bắt
vì có tiền Mẹ "đút lót người công an"

Tuổi thơ tôi, chứng kiến những cảnh:
người từ "vùng kinh tế mới" về mất nhà cửa, ở gầm cầu . . .
Và chỉ nghe những từ ngữ "làm lậu" "đút lót" "ăn chia" . . .

Và xa hơn nữa, những cảnh "hối lộ" ngất ngưỡng muôn trùng . . .

Tuổi thơ tôi, ai đã lấy

—TH (April 2005)
[viết cho tuổi thơ đã mất . . .]

Days and months passed. The tears dried up
Because of crying. I missed my Mom and Dad.

When I was young, I was scared
Worried that night by night
The police came to capture my brother as "young volunteers" invaded Kampuchea

Since then, I was nervous
When I heard dogs barking far away in other alleys
Quietly in the dark night . . .
I knew my brother was safe another night
Because Mom paid money to the police for "bribery rules"

My childhood, witnessed
Homeless people from the "subsidized economy" came
Back, lost home and all, lived under bridges for home.
All I heard was bribery, black markets . . .

Further . . . further . . . more, everywhere bribery rising high like a mountain.

My childhood, that was my childhood

—Thuhang (April 2005)
[For the loss of my childhood]

PART I

Thuhang

CHAPTER 1

Shattered Dreams

Memories of April 1975 are seared into my brain like a branding iron stamped on the flesh of a cow. I remember the events vividly, as if they happened yesterday. My heart thunderously pounds in my chest as I share my story with you.

My new rattan suitcase with red leather trim sat in the corner of the living room. It was filled to the brim with hope of a new life.

Mom and I had spent several days shopping for new clothes for my trip to West Germany. She carefully packed each item with love and care. My favorite outfit was a big orange-and-white polka-dot shirt and pants. This colorful, cool pantsuit was the last item packed. Mom placed my travel documents on top of my mod-looking outfit. I was scheduled to leave Saigon on June 14, 1975.

I needed to be brave. I was five years old, and I was going to travel from Saigon to West Germany for polio rehabilitation therapy. My leg muscles had atrophied, and my left leg bent at an odd angle, like a broken pencil, as I crawled along the floor. My clothing had ragged holes in the knees from my aggressive movements to keep up with my older brother, Quang Phuong, my sister, Linh Phuong, and the neighborhood kids.

I was forced to crawl awkwardly like an infant while I yearned to run free and fast like other children. I used to walk and run until I developed a high fever at age two and a half. My siblings and I had been vaccinated for polio, but when I became ill, my leg muscles weakened. My parents were shocked when the doctor said that I had contracted paralytic polio.

Dad constantly researched polio treatments with the hope that I would someday walk again. I tried acupuncture and monthly electric shock treatments, *chay dien*, to activate my leg nerves. Nothing helped. Dad heard about the Kenny regimen, a new polio treatment involving hot, moist packs with exercises to strengthen unaffected muscles. A West German foundation provided this revolutionary Kenny treatment. My family and I were ecstatic when I was accepted into the program.

Dad was an air traffic controller in the South Vietnam Air Force. He spent his military career helping the South Vietnam and US Air Force special units in "hot spots" during the Vietnam War. He had been stationed at military bases in Da Nang and Saigon. His last assignment was at the Can Tho Air Force Base, which is eighty miles south of Saigon.

We lived in a town close to the Tan Son Nhat airport in Saigon called Xom Choi Long Ga, in the Go Vap district. Dad came home on his days off by catching a ride on a plane or helicopter from Can Tho to Saigon. Dad's brother, my Uncle Dinh, lived with us. He was much younger than Dad; he was only fourteen years old in 1975.

My brother Quang Phuong is five years older than me. His name means "clear direction" or "horizon." He charts his own course and stubbornly takes a different path. The name Phuong can be used for boys or girls. It is pronounced with a different enunciation depending on gender. Phuong for a male means "one who knows his destiny." Quang Phuong is a spitting image of Dad. When I developed polio, my brother became very protective of me.

My sister Linh Phuong is three years older than me, and as young children, we were inseparable. Phuong for girls references the phoenix bird, a sacred mythical creature in the Old Testament that rises out of the ashes. Linh means "gentle spirit." Linh Phuong always has a smile on her face, and she bends over backward to be understanding, conciliatory, and flexible. Growing up, she often observed Quang Phuong's approach and then tried something dramatically different. Mom dressed me and Linh Phuong in matching outfits when we could afford them.

I am the youngest in my family. My name is Thu Hang, which means "full moon." My parents chose my name hoping my life would be full and bright like the moon at *Tet Trung Thu*, the mid-autumn moon festival.

Mom's name is Lieu, which means "willow"; she is soft and beautiful on the outside but strong and resilient on the inside. Mom and Dad met during the Vietnam War. Mom cooked and served *banh cuon*, steamed rice rolls with ground meat, at an outdoor market booth. Dad was a regular customer who worked up his courage to ask her on a date. Dad's name, Chinh, means "righteous." He has strong morals, ethics, and integrity.

Mom and Dad were a great team. Mom was an excellent cook; she stayed home and took great care of her family. Dad was a proud, hardworking, intelligent man who thrived on learning new things.

My parents had similar backgrounds. Dad's mother passed away when he was a teenager, and Mom's father died when she was a teen. Both of my parents experienced the horrors of the First Indochina War, also known as the Franco-Viet Minh War. Their families migrated to South Vietnam in 1954 when the country was divided in two. My parents were devout Catholics and passionate about democracy.

We visited Dad many times at the different military bases, and I loved the tours he gave us. He always picked me up and carried me; he treated me like a princess. I couldn't wait to see him and feel his strong, protective arms around me. My favorite game was called airplane. Dad threw me high in the air when an airplane was taking off. I felt like I was in flight! He caught me as I landed in his strong arms. We both laughed hysterically, and I begged him to do it again: "Please, Daddy, throw me up in the air again!" He made me feel special. He made me feel loved.

When we visited Dad at the air base, he told me, my brother, and my sister about the various airplanes—many were from the United States, like the North American T-6 Texans, the Douglas A-1 Skyraiders, and the planes known as Bird Dogs. The Sikorsky H-10 helicopters looked like huge dragonflies. We laughed when he told us the nicknames of some of the helicopters—one was called the Jolly Green Giant because it held many soldiers, another was called Cross-Eyed Monster, and the one that lifted and carried heavy loads was named Skycrane.

During one of our visits to the base, Dad took us on a tour of the city on a cyclo, a type of tricycle that was a uniquely Vietnamese mode of transportation. It was a three-wheeled bicycle with a passenger compartment up front. When we stopped and got off the cyclo, I remember that Dad began kissing Mom, and I started teasing them. Then I moved away to give them some private time. I watched people walking on the street. Dad knew that I had given them some rare, precious time together, so when he picked me up, he started tickling me, and I began giggling.

But the month of April 1975 felt very different compared to the previous months. We had not visited Dad at the air base in quite a while. The air of excitement that had filled our home for the past few weeks in preparation for my trip to West Germany changed drastically. I didn't know much about the fighting oc-curring in the cities and countryside. Saigon had been relatively peaceful during most of the war. However, lately, many refugees had arrived in the city.

Mom was seriously distressed. Her face contorted with worry while she talked in hushed tones with our neighbors. She seemed unable to focus and frequently wrung her hands. With Dad eighty miles away at work, Mom was responsible for her three young children and her husband's teenage brother.

I overheard our neighbors talking quietly about Hue and Da Nang. I knew that Dad wasn't at Da Nang anymore, but it terrified me to hear that his old military base had surrendered to the enemy. Mom tried to reassure me that Dad was safe because his military base was the farthest south. What I didn't know was that Can Tho had been aggressively attacked by the Viet Cong recently. The center of Can Tho had been bombarded with rockets and intense artillery exchanges. Mom didn't tell me that she'd tried to visit Dad in Can Tho the week before but was unable to make it due to a Viet Cong checkpoint. Mom tried to hide her concerns from us, but we sensed that she was extremely worried.

If I could have looked at a map, I would have seen that the Viet Cong had conquered all of the country north of Saigon. The Viet Cong were moving rapidly from the eastern Cambodian border into an area south of Saigon and north of Can Tho. The city of Saigon was being encircled by Communist troops.

We began hearing thunderous bombs and explosions along with the wailing of sirens in the early morning hours of April 29. I was petrified and frozen in my spot. I was not sure what to do, and Mom looked like a lost child. Our burly neighbor banged on our door, came running inside, and began digging a shelter under our kitchen floor, close to our front door. Mom and Uncle Dinh immediately began helping him dig.

Mom yelled to my brother Quang Phuong to break the legs off of one of our kitchen chairs. Our neighbor grabbed a hammer and nails and quickly constructed a crude ladder for our shelter. Uncle Dinh noisily climbed on our roof and, with the help of other neighbors, ripped off two sheets of metal, which were placed on top of the shelter. After several hours of digging, we had a hiding place that would hopefully keep us safe from bombs, mortar fire, and enemy soldiers. Homemade shelters in Vietnam were called *hams*.

As we were scrambling to create a safe place, the walls of our home shook violently each time a bomb exploded. I felt like I was the only one who noticed because everyone else was so intently focused on digging and searching for items to include in and on top of the *ham*. The terrifying explosions were punctuated by periods of deathly silence. Then the staccato of machine guns started, and people began screaming.

Once the bunker was deep and wide enough for five of us to fit, Mom laid down one small bamboo mat to keep us from getting covered with clammy, soft dirt. She carried a kerosene lantern down the rickety handmade steps, and we huddled together. My entire body was shaking uncontrollably as fear and adrenaline coursed through my veins.

Uncle Dinh was the last person in the *ham*. He placed two large metal sheets over the top of the bunker. Once the *ham* was covered, the air became hot and sticky, and it felt like living inside a coffin. I felt like I was suffocating and couldn't breathe, but I didn't dare complain.

The noises outside were horrendous. There were deafening explosions that shook the ground like a never-ending earthquake. We heard artillery shells dropping on our rooftop, and it seemed like our home was going to crumble and bury us alive. Then it became eerily quiet and still. We were unsure if we should come out of the bunker. Each time we thought about venturing out of the *ham*, another rocket exploded nearby.

Fear paralyzed us. We didn't speak or cry. Mom constantly prayed with her rosary; her lips moved, but no sound came out.

Prayers seemed to be our only hope. We didn't talk about Dad and where he might be. I imagined he was fighting off the enemy and winning. I prayed silently and often for his safety.

After spending most of the day in the *ham*, we crawled out of the deep, dark hole to find food. Very little food was in the house, so we needed to ration it to last several days for five of us. Mom placed a small rice ball sprinkled with ground, roasted peanuts and sesame seeds in my outstretched hand. She warned me to eat it slowly because it might be my only food for several days. I placed my rice ball in my pocket and only pulled it out when my hunger pains were beating my stomach like a large bass drum.

Uncle Dinh ventured outside for a few minutes but returned shaking and sobbing. He said, "There are dead bodies out there." He mentioned that he saw several enemy soldiers crawling out of tunnels in the streets of our neighborhood. Mom held Dinh close to calm him down.

With the news of Viet Cong soldiers in our neighborhood, Quang Phuong, Uncle Dinh, and Mom moved heavier furniture near the entrance of the *ham*. They wanted it harder for the enemy to get to us in the shelter, so they arranged dressers, bed frames, and chairs in a circle around the *ham*. The furniture that functioned as sentries could take some direct hits from shrapnel and artillery, if need be.

Intense curiosity caused me to peer out of the window during a time of eerie silence. The sky looked like it was on fire; huge billows of dense grey smoke danced alongside tremendous, raging red flames. The smell of burnt vegetation, charred homes, and pungent, unknown odors wafted through my nostrils. I didn't see any of our neighbors. I didn't hear a sound. The homes around us looked like shell-shocked survivors with gaping holes in their sides and personal belongings littering the streets. It was a ghost town.

My throat felt dry and raspy because I hadn't had anything to drink. Mom warned us to only drink rainwater because our well water was probably contaminated from the dead bodies on the ground. It hadn't rained yet, so the bowl she set out to capture rainwater was bone dry.

We stayed inside the house near the entrance to the *ham* and bolted into our hiding place when we heard sirens, explosions, or artillery. Because I couldn't move quickly, Mom picked me up and threw me down the entrance; I landed in my uncle's or brother's arms. We moved fast to stay safe and alive.

Darkness magnified my fears. The terrifying noises seemed much closer than before. I imagined that there were rats and snakes in the bunker. I barely slept, and, when I did drift off, I was awakened by nightmares about Dad being killed by the Viet Cong. I also dreamt that I drank contaminated water and became a grotesque zombie. I wasn't sure if my current reality or my nightmares were worse. Mom tried to comfort us by hugging us tight and squeezing our hands. My sister, Linh Phuong, and I clung to each other in terror. Words were not necessary.

On the morning of April 30, we crawled out of the *ham* when we hadn't heard any artillery chatter from the M-16s and AK-47s or any overhead screaming rockets for several hours. We quickly used the bathroom and began searching for scraps of food in the kitchen. We shared some dried instant noodles, a stale piece of bread, and a rotten guava.

Suddenly, our neighbor burst into our house carrying his Sony transistor radio. "Hurry, President Minh is about to make an important announcement. Come over to my house to listen." As we walked outside, we gagged on the acrid smell of explosives. Our family quickly arrived next door and crowded into his home, which already had many neighbors, friends, and relatives packed inside.

At 10:24 a.m., the radio crackled to life as President Duong Van Minh addressed the listeners. President Minh had become the South Vietnamese president forty-eight hours earlier after President Nguyen Van Thieu was forced to resign, fled Vietnam, and blamed the United States for betraying South Vietnam by not providing military aid and funding that he felt had been promised.

President Minh's radio announcement of unconditional surrender was brief. "I believe firmly in reconciliation among Vietnamese to avoid unnecessary shedding of the blood of Vietnamese. For this reason, I ask the soldiers of the Republic of Vietnam to cease hostilities in calm and to stay where they are."[1]

At five years old, I didn't understand what was being said on the radio until someone yelled, "The war is over!" Some people were crying, some were cheering, and others sat in stunned silence. Mom gasped loudly, and all of the color drained from her face.

The radio announcer described the chaotic scene in Saigon from the day before, when last-minute helicopter evacuations occurred from the grounds of the US Embassy. Thousands of South

Vietnamese had surrounded the wall of the embassy and were desperate to be one of the lucky ones chosen to fly to freedom.

The radio announcer's voice went up several octaves as he announced that a Viet Cong tank had just smashed through the elaborately decorated steel gates of the presidential palace. A single soldier ran across the palace grounds carrying the flag of our enemy: crimson red on top and blue on the bottom with a bright yellow star in the middle. The announcer mentioned that the design of the flag, according to the Viet Cong, was blue for the peaceful North and red for the bloody South, and the yellow star in the middle symbolized the unity of all yellow-skinned people in Vietnam. The flag was hoisted up and flown from the presidential palace. Then the streets of Saigon were flooded with Viet Cong tanks, trucks, and troops weary and intoxicated with victory.

As we walked back into our home, I noticed that the heart of my small rattan suitcase had been pierced by shrapnel. The guts of my dreams were strewn with clothing and rubbish on the floor.

In the flash of an instant, our entire world had turned upside down on April 30, 1975.

CHAPTER 2

Luat Rung: Jungle Law

The darkest day in South Vietnam, April 30, 1975, goes by many names. South Vietnamese refer to this day as Black April, *Thang Tu Den*, or National Day of Resentment. North Vietnamese call it Liberation Day, and Westerners refer to it as the Fall of Saigon.

In the late afternoon on April 30, 1975, the shrill ring of the telephone broke the heavy silence in our home. I closely watched Uncle Dinh trying to mask his conversation on the phone. He was listening intently and hardly speaking. When he did say something into the phone, he spoke in a soft, barely audible whisper.

After Uncle Dinh finished talking on the phone, he pulled Mom aside to talk with her. The look on Mom's face stopped us in our tracks. She was deathly pale; her eyes were cold, hard steel; and her hands shook. "What's wrong, Mom?" we asked. She insisted that everything was fine and told us to be very quiet.

We knew that something serious had happened or was happening. Mom began setting aside some clothing for each of us. She hurriedly stuffed the items that she had chosen into an old, brown, tired-looking leather suitcase. There were two frayed straps that wrapped around the worn case. One of the suitcase latches failed to catch and kept protruding out in defiance.

Mom grabbed the scissors and cut a small opening at the top of the hem in her pants. We watched in astonished silence as she opened her jewelry box and placed some of her jewelry in the fold of her pants. She rapidly stitched around each piece of jewelry so that it did not make a sound when she walked.

Then Mom told us that Dad was coming home to pick us up and take us to the airport. Under normal circumstances, the drive took Dad about an hour and a half. We waited, and we waited.

Time crawled painfully toward eternity.

While waiting for Dad to come home and pick us up, I said many prayers of thanks to God for keeping Dad safe. I closed my eyes and cherished thoughts of him.

Dad was my hero. I was the first person he went to every time he walked into our house. He always picked me up and carried me wherever he went. He would tell Mom that we were going for a walk in the neighborhood. Then he'd show me off and talk about how proud he was of me while we chatted with our neighbors. He made me glow.

My dad was also my hero because he fought for independence and freedom for South Vietnam. He was extremely proud of his country and always said that he would fight to the end to defend against communism. Dad ardently believed in freedom of speech and freedom of thought. He mentioned that if South Vietnam fell to the Communists, our abilities to pursue our dreams, education, and career choices, as well as the ability to express our own thoughts, would be stifled. I wondered what he was thinking now.

I liked bragging to my friends about Dad's strength and brav-
ery. His determination and courage sparked a fire in me to be just
like him. He had an infectious smile on his face, and his positive,
can-do attitude inspired me. He set high expectations for each of
his children, and I did not want to disappoint him.

The intensity of the war determined how frequently we got
to see Dad. Whenever he could, he came home on his days off.
He always carried his dark-blue hard-case valise and set it down
immediately inside the front door when he arrived. One time, I
asked him why he called it a valise, and he told me that *valise* was
the French word for suitcase. Dad's father, Grandpa Ong Noi, spoke
three languages: French, Thai, and Vietnamese. Every now and then,
Dad used a French or Thai word I didn't understand. I said the word
valise over and over because it had a funny, lyrical sound to it.

Sometimes, I admired and touched the cold steel engraved
nameplate on his valise that said *Tran Van Chinh* in crisp block
letters. His name looked important and official. In Vietnamese tradition, the last name appears first (Tran), followed by the middle
name. The person's first name (Chinh) is listed last.

If I knew that Dad was coming home, I sat outside at the base
of our well in our front yard, waiting for him. I kept a lookout for
his blue hard-case valise to swing into my ground-level view. Then
I lifted my head high to see into his face as he scooped me into
his big, protective, strong arms. He hugged and kissed me as he
carried me inside the house. He always asked if I had been a good
girl and wondered what I had been doing. He looked deep into my
eyes and listened intently.

The weekends Dad came home were the best times in the world. As a family, we talked and played games. Dad usually brought home spicy sauces or fresh fruit like mangos, bananas, or apricots that Mom used immediately. Mom often cooked sticky rice with red fruit inside called *xoi gac*.

The moment our neighbors knew that Dad was home, they came over to talk with him. The men talked about politics and the war. The two girls across the alley asked Dad's advice about school. The neighborhood girls were older than my brother, and they viewed my father like an uncle. In Vietnamese culture, men were called "uncle" as a term of endearment or friendship rather than as a reference to being a relative.

Sometimes, after dinner, Dad lay on the hammock with Linh Phuong and me on each side of him. Dad taught us to sing some of his favorite Vietnamese songs. We loved singing the songs while gently swaying in the hammock. One time, he asked me to sing in front of his friends; they were surprised and in awe.

My mind shifted away from memories of Dad to the clear and present moment. We had been waiting for hours for Dad to come home and take us to the airport. Darkness settled like an oppressive blanket inside our home. No one said a word. We sat and waited.

Dad never arrived home. Dejected beyond words, we spent the night of April 30, 1975, in our deep, dank cell beneath our kitchen floor. No one spoke. No one cried. We were in a state of catatonic shock.

The next day, we heard soldiers marching in the alleys near our home and looked outside. After the soldiers passed, I noticed a horrific sight that is forever singed in my memory. It was a deep hole stacked full of dead bodies. Flies swarmed around like a dense, thick carpet of black fog. The dead included soldiers from both sides, civilians, babies, elders, and even dogs. There were guns, grenades, ammunition, and any identifying item that symbolized the South Vietnam Army.

The smell of death from the decomposing bodies outside our window permeated our skin and lungs. There were many mass gravesites and warehouses filled with corpses. It felt like death was knocking at our door and whispering to come inside.

My world erupted into chaos. Neighbors cried and searched for their loved ones in the pile of dead bodies. Looting broke out, particularly at food locations, including the food distribution center for the South Vietnam Army. My uncle and my brother looted to find food for our family. They brought me some M&M candies and comic books they stole.

By the first of May, all phone lines were destroyed, and phone communication ceased in Saigon. It felt like Saigon was in a dead zone. Mom believed that Dad was stuck at the Can Tho Air Force Base. She asked her two brothers, my Uncle Xuan and Uncle Truc, to locate Dad based on people they knew, but they couldn't find Dad. Nor could they find anyone who had seen him.

While trying to locate Dad, we also searched for relatives to make sure they were safe. Mom grew up in a large, boisterous family with three brothers and two sisters. Mom's mother, my Grandma Ba Ngoai, lived with her son Truc and his family.

Mom's sister, Aunt Kim, and her husband and twin sons lived nearby. Mom's relatives were shaken by the events, but they were all safe.

Dad's father, my Grandpa Ong Noi, lived in the Central Highlands area, approximately five hundred miles away, so it took a long time to hear that Grandpa was safe. Dad's only sibling, Uncle Dinh, lived with us. Days and weeks passed; no one heard from Dad or knew his whereabouts.

Life was moving in slow motion. Dad was constantly on my mind as I worried about him. Where was he? Was he safe? Was he alive? Was he ever coming home? Mom's demeanor vacillated between sharp tones and gut-wrenching sobs. Our family had been blown to smithereens.

Every day, our neighbor came over with his Sony transistor radio, or we went to his house to listen to Radio Saigon, *Dai phat thanh Sai Gon*. There were large public speakers mounted on top of telephone poles in downtown Saigon, where we heard public messages. Televisions were extremely rare.

According to one radio broadcast, a Communist party was formed called CSVN, *Dang Cong San Vietnam*, shortened to *Cong San*. Cong San was given control of all South Vietnamese property, real estate, businesses, and the lives and activities of civilians. CSVN policemen, *Cong An*, went to each neighborhood and rounded up people to read new rules to them.

Cong San immediately took possession of personal property. As they forced residents from their homes, residents were told that their property was *my nguy*, which meant the property had belonged to South Vietnam or the Americans, and now it belonged to the Communists. Hundreds of thousands of people immediately became homeless.

Luckily, our small, modest house with mortar damage did not interest the new regime. Uncle Truc and his family moved to Bien Hoa Dong Nai when their home was confiscated by the Communists. Grandma Ba Ngoai came to live with us after Uncle Truc's home was taken. Aunt Kim, her husband, and their twin sons lived across the alley from our home; fortunately, their home was not confiscated.

Communist actions seemed contradictory. They continually spoke about people being equal and everyone being a farmer or laborer, yet, at the same time, they viciously grabbed and kept expensive homes, cars, art, jewelry, and personal belongings. They were drunk on the excesses of life that they confiscated.

The Viet Cong wanted to obliterate everything about South Vietnam. They fought long and hard for thirty years to create one unified Vietnam. They immediately bulldozed hundreds of thousands of graves in all South Vietnamese military cemeteries. We were ordered to burn any papers, videos, artwork, books, and photographs related to *my nguy*, South Vietnam, or America. Mom was terrified *Cong An* would put her in jail if she didn't follow Communist orders. Mom created a small fire in a metal can in our backyard. She sharply asked us to collect all photographs and books and help her burn them.

"Mom, I want to keep some photos of Dad and our family," I begged.

"No! No! If I don't follow the rules, *Cong An* will put me in jail—then who will take care of you?"

"How will I remember what Dad looks like? I want to keep one or two photos," I wailed.

"Absolutely not! We want to stay alive, so everything must be burnt. *Cong An* will kill us if we don't obey them. Now go get all of the photos, quickly."

While Mom was busy collecting items to burn, I quickly hid several photos of Dad and our family in a small tin can. Later, I buried the tin can in the corner of the kitchen close to the *ham*. Now that the Communists were in charge, we didn't use our *ham*, and I knew that Mom wouldn't notice the small area tucked behind the kitchen cabinet near the *ham* entrance where my secret photos were hidden.

To obliterate everything related to South Vietnam and to honor senior Viet Cong officials, the names of cities, streets, and buildings in South Vietnam were renamed. Saigon became Ho Chi Minh City. Tu Do Street was renamed Dong Khoi. Not only were street names changed, but the specific numbering of addresses was completely changed as well. It was as if every city, every street, and every home was captured, conquered, and reborn as a Communist place.

The Communists closed all businesses. Then they created a registration process where each business was registered with the new government and existed under government control. This socialist business model was called the subsidy period, *Thoi Bao Cap*. To reclaim their previously owned businesses, citizens had to pay exorbitant license fees. The new regime determined how each business was run. In most instances, Communists ran the business, and the owner was given the lowest-level position within their own business, such as a dishwasher in a restaurant.

Each neighborhood was assigned a Communist watch person called a cell leader. Cell leaders watched for reactionary conversations and behaviors. Communists only trusted other Communists. Cell leaders held indoctrination meetings three times a week that all civilians were required to attend. These mandatory meetings included discussions about Ho Chi Minh and the benefits of communism. Neighbors and family members were quick to tell on each other by informing cell leaders about suspicious behaviors. Trust was eroded, and silence became the norm.

Frequent loudspeaker broadcasts touted Communist Party slogans and propaganda. In some cities, broadcast speakers woke citizens at 4:30 a.m. with instructions on exercise. The government became involved in all aspects of our lives: work, play, family, school, religion, and cultural traditions.

Initially, the Communists eliminated the Tet holiday as well as Christmas. For Vietnamese, the Tet Nguyen Dan festival is our Lunar New Year celebration. Vietnamese all celebrate their birthdays on Tet, and everyone is one year older, regardless of their actual birthday. We strongly believe that the first visitor who crosses the threshold in our home after midnight on Tet must be of good character or the family will have an unlucky year.

During Tet, we honor our ancestors and deceased loved ones. Each home has a family altar where photos of deceased relatives are placed in their honor. The altar is decorated with flowers, fruit, candles, and incense. Paper charms are hung throughout the home to ward off evil spirits. In each home, the eldest male greets the spirits that are arriving from heaven by placing rice cakes and soybean soup on the ancestral altar. He blesses the celebration, and the feast begins.

Despite the new regime's order to not recognize Tet or Christmas, some citizens continued to practice their religious and cultural customs with discretion. Several years later, the bans against Tet and Christmas were eliminated.

One of the most degrading acts was standing in line to exchange our South Vietnamese currency, the *dong*. Providing our money to the Communists was called *Doi Tien*, money exchange. It wasn't based on an exchange rate but was based on the number of people in each household. It was complete robbery. Instead of currency, we were given a food stamp booklet, *So Gao Tem Phieu*. The food stamps were not enough to provide food for us to survive. But who could we voice our concerns to?

It seemed like the world had gone mad, and we lived under jungle law, *luat rung*.

Little did I know that my world would be ripped asunder several times throughout my life.

CHAPTER 3

My Fallen Hero

Three long, arduous months had passed since the beautiful city of Saigon was captured. I witnessed Mom transform from a gorgeous, spirit-filled, optimistic lover of life into a woman terrified of everything due to the new rules and policies of the Communists.

One day, there was a loud, persistent knock on our front door. When Mom opened the door, she gasped and took a step backward. My father's friend, Uncle Dat, stood uncomfortably in the doorway, holding Dad's blue hard-case valise with the engraved nameplate I had touched and read so many times. Uncle Dat gingerly stepped into the house and set Dad's valise in the exact spot where Dad had always placed it.

Uncle Dat gently embraced Mom. With tears flowing down his face, he sobbed, "I'm so sorry."

Mom started to shake uncontrollably and wailed, "He can't be gone. Chinh can't be gone."

In a quiet, trembling voice, Mom asked him to explain exactly what happened to Dad. He said that Dad had climbed aboard a helicopter with wing number 790 at the Can Tho Air Force Base in the late afternoon of April 30, 1975. The situation was getting dire by the minute. Uncle Dat described soldiers and civilians clutching the wheel wells of airplanes and helicopters and falling to their deaths.

Uncle Dat said that he and Dad exchanged final words in the hallway before Dad headed to the helicopter. Dad said, "If you find my family, please let them know that I am safe, and I am going to the United States with my troops."

Uncle Dat mentioned that he had spent the next thirty minutes talking with other comrades about their plans for evacuating or staying in Vietnam. Then he had looked out the window and noticed that the helicopter with wing number 790 was overloaded with passengers. The helicopter bounced along the tarmac and had trouble gaining altitude for liftoff. It rose into the sky and started lurching and sputtering. With horror, Uncle Dat saw the Huey helicopter fall from the sky into the nearby river and erupt in flames.

Uncle Dat said that Dad's suitcase and other people's belongings fell out of the helicopter upon impact. Some items dropped into the river, while others flew into the air and landed on the riverbank. Dad's valise was recovered from the riverbank.

Uncle Dat embraced Mom while she cried, and he continually said, "I'm sorry, I am so sorry." My brother, sister, and I sat beside Mom with big tears running down our cheeks.

After Uncle Dat left, I lovingly looked at Dad's suitcase, which had represented joy and happiness each time he walked into our home and set it down. I was filled with immense sorrow. I would never feel his strong, protective arms around me. He wouldn't be lifting me in the air to play the airplane game. I wanted to cherish his love, his laugh, and his belief in me.

Dad's dark-blue hard-case valise had some deep scratches on the surface, but it was undamaged and still intact. Mom clicked open the latches and looked inside. She pulled out our birth certificates and slowly looked at each one as tears welled up in her eyes. Spasmodic sobs shook her body when she pulled out their marriage license. She set the suitcase aside, unable to continue looking at the contents.

Later that night, I snuck Dad's suitcase to my bedroom and peered inside. I noticed several family photos. One photo was Dad at the Da Nang air traffic control tower. There were also several changes of clothing, along with Dad's military hat, tucked neatly within the folds of one of his crisp military shirts. I held on to his photo and military hat and sobbed uncontrollably as I lay on the floor.

The next day, our home was filled with grieving relatives, neighbors, and friends. Grandma Ba Ngoai, Aunt Kim, and our cousins cried and hugged all of us. Uncle Xuan and Uncle Truc offered to help Mom with the funeral arrangements.

Although we didn't have my father's body to bury, we wanted to give him a traditional Vietnamese burial rite with Mass, *Le Phat Tang*. The funeral service was held at our church, Giao Xu Hoang Mai. We placed a large photo of Dad wearing civilian clothes, not his military uniform, on our family altar, along with flowers and burning diffuser sticks in scented agarwood—*cay giang*—oil. The aroma was musky, woodsy, and masculine. It seeped into my nostrils like wisps of memories.

As is customary, our family wore white clothing without jewelry for the first three days of mourning. The color white represented the ashes of the deceased. As a widow, Mom wore a white pointed hood with oversized white pants and a tunic that symbolized sorrow and loss. Mom's face was as pale as her clothing.

After the funeral, I asked Mom if I could keep Dad's blue hard-case valise in my room. I wanted to keep him as close to me as possible. Each night before I fell asleep, I pulled his photo out of his valise and talked with him. I told him how much I missed him. I asked him what life was like in heaven and if he was happy. During my bleakest days, I felt comforted at night when I looked at his photo and spoke to him. I hoped that he could hear me.

In Vietnamese tradition, for three years after Dad's death, each of our family members wore a small black or white checker-size square piece of fabric attached to our collars that signified we were in mourning. In addition to wearing the fabric on our collars, we also followed the norms of public mourning by wearing customary white headbands around our foreheads for three years.

Our mourning process, *song goi thac ve,* recognized that our father's new spirit would come and occupy our home. Our culture believes that if a person dies away from their home, their soul wanders the countryside until prayers guide it back home. My grandma, uncles, aunts, neighbors, and friends prayed for Dad's soul to be in a good place with God.

As is customary, we continued prayer sessions for the first fifty days after the news about my father's death. We held prayer sessions each week at our house, with relatives, neighbors, and friends continuing to pray for Dad's soul to be at peace and in heaven. On each year's anniversary of his death, we held a memorial service at our church, and the entire congregation prayed for Dad's soul.

After three years of mourning had passed, our family, relatives, neighbors, and friends attended Mass at church and prayed again for Dad's soul. We followed Vietnamese tradition and burnt the mourning clothes, white headbands, and small checker-size cloths. This ceremony recognized that Dad's soul had gone to heaven and that, as a family, we could move on with our lives.

Our neighbors, friends, and relatives comforted us during our time of grief. Many felt sympathy for Mom as a young woman with three children and no husband. But it was a brief respite because our world had changed so drastically and many others had lost husbands, brothers, and sons in the war.

The best we could do was to continue trying to survive one more day.

CHAPTER 4

High-Voltage Hardship

I thought Dad dying was the worst thing that could happen to me. His death was just a preface of the continual high-voltage hardships my family and I endured.

In addition to the seizing of all personal property, the closing of businesses, and the rationing of food, many Southerners were sent to isolated reeducation camps, *Trai Hoc Tap Cai Tao*. The new Communist regime encouraged all men who had served the South Vietnamese government and military to come forward and complete paperwork. Once they completed the paperwork, these men were told that they would be sent to reeducation camps for ten to thirty days and then released.

Hundreds of thousands of men came forward, believing what they had been told. It was the last time many of them saw their loved ones because they were transported to remote areas where reeducation camps were located. Religious leaders, educators, and professionals were also rounded up and exported to these camps. These weren't reeducation camps; they were prisons where the prisoners were forced into hard labor, tortured, beaten, and killed.

Our neighbor who always shared his Sony transistor radio programs with us had two sons who were sent to reeducation camps in

29

the North. His sons' wives and children begged and pleaded to be able to say goodbye but were brusquely told no by *Cong An*.

Once many of the men had been sent away to these camps, the new Communist government forced all adults and children who were able to work to join the economic program *Vung Kinh Te Moi*. The economic program was basically centralized agriculture. Hundreds of thousands of South Vietnamese were forced to give their homes to Communist Party leaders and leave Saigon to begin farming for the government.

My mom, sister, and brother and thousands of other families were forced to leave their homes and ancestral villages and march to the empty, damaged lands in the Trang Bom area. Trang Bom was about 275 miles southeast of Saigon; it was where some of the most intense fighting had occurred during the war. They farmed with their bare hands because they didn't own any farming tools, and none were provided by the government.

Because of my disability and age, I did not have to participate in the economic program. I lived with Grandma Ba Ngoai and Aunt Kim. My grandma was too old to work in the fields, and my aunt was excused from farming because her twin sons were toddlers.

Before farming could begin, the removal of dead bodies, debris, weapons, ammunitions, and trash was necessary. There were live mines and booby traps throughout the countryside that had been created during the war. Some villagers lost legs, arms, or their lives when they began digging up the land for farming.

Housing was nonexistent. A fellow farmer helped Mom construct a lean-to shelter with coconut leaves for the roof. My mom, brother, and sister slept on the ground huddled together for warmth and comfort. When it rained, which was often, the water soaked them to the bone, and the floor became thick mud. Mom relied on neighbors and friends to help her while farming, and she reciprocated often.

My mom, brother, and sister grew several different crops: corn, squash, green beans, and peas. Once the crops were harvested, the large majority of the proceeds went to the Communist government. The remaining proceeds were divided among all farming citizens.

I did not see Mom during the time she was forced into being a farm laborer. Being separated from my family at five years old was terrifying. Grandma tried to comfort me, but I missed Dad, Mom, Quang Phuong, and Linh Phuong so badly. I quietly cried myself to sleep at night.

There were few children in our neighborhood because most went to the farmlands with their parents. Due to polio, I crawled on the ground to move. My playmates were insects; I was fascinated watching ants, grasshoppers, and crickets.

While watching the ants march purposefully, I started thinking about Dad. I missed his smile and infectious positive attitude. He brightened up any room he entered. Dad seemed purposeful, like the ants working so hard on the ground. I wondered what Dad would do if he were in my situation.

I thought about how sad my grandma and aunt seemed all of the time. They rarely smiled. Then I realized that I could be the sunshine in their lives. Rather than whining and crying, I could try to bring joy and happiness to our lives. I didn't want to be viewed as a burden, so I started thinking about how I could help. My aunt's twin boys were two years old—I could play with them and show them the insects that fascinated me. I began thinking of other ways I could help, such as gathering plants for cooking and finding ways to make my grandma and aunt smile occasionally. This shift in perspective helped me get through some of my bleakest moments.

Food was very scarce, and it was rationed by the government. I typically ate only corn or rice for each meal without any protein or anything else. Each night, I went to sleep hungry due to lack of food. My stomach contractions from hunger pains were excruciating and often kept me from sleeping.

Sometimes, I ate food that was rotten because I was constantly starving. I was so hungry that any type of food looked appealing. Due to malnourishment, my belly became swollen. I looked like a pregnant child. My arms and legs were rail thin, and my ribs protruded above my swollen belly. I was always sick, but medicine and doctors were not available for citizens treated as lowly peasants nor to people who were not members of the Communist Party.

After one year of centralized agriculture, most of the crops were lost due to lack of water, no fertilization, and corruption from the government. Harvesting stopped. My mom, brother, and sister moved back to Saigon. It felt good to have all of us under the same roof again.

After families returned from farming, many lived under bridges and in alleyways because they were homeless. Beggars became commonplace, and orphaned children roamed the streets looking for food and selling lottery tickets and cigarettes to help their families survive another day. Many children became illiterate.

I remember gorging myself on fresh corn on the cob Mom brought home from farming. I loved it because it had been so long since I had tasted fresh food. A rare delicacy for our meals was being able to add a few peanuts cooked in a fish sauce over our rice. We savored every bite and licked our bowls clean. Occasionally, we had sweet potatoes we found in other yards, or we had an egg we would heavily salt and split up to use over several days.

Once Mom was back home, she attempted to fix up our house. It was damaged during the bombing in Saigon, and little had been done during the time she was away farming in the countryside. Since we didn't need the *ham* anymore, she focused on filling in the bunker and repairing the kitchen with the help of our neighbors. I knew that I needed to move my tin can that held the hidden photos. One day, when Mom was at the market, I removed the tin can and placed it deep inside Dad's blue hard-case valise.

As a family, we did many different types of work to survive. Mom sold grains of rice. She rode her bicycle to the marketplace far from Saigon called Xa Cang Mien Tay and purchased a large, fifty-pound bag of rice and then resold it by the kernel and by the pint. When she rode back from the marketplace, she rode her bike on desolate back roads to avoid being questioned by the Communist police, *Cong An*. She sold the rice in our alley, from within our home, and at the nearby market.

Within each alley in our community, every family had a role in the production assembly line. Our alley was nicknamed the

"Chicken Feather" alley, *Xom Choi Long Ga*. One family sorted chicken feathers by size and color. Another family washed and cut bamboo sticks. The next family applied the asphalt-type glue to the bottom of the bamboo stick.

Our family's role was placing the feathers on the glued area of the bamboo stick and then connecting the feathers together with needle and thread. I became adept at this chore despite the hardened callouses on my hands. The finished product was a feather duster.

We also dyed some of the white chicken feathers different colors and made decorative items for homes and for artistic performances. Although the work was tedious and repetitive, it was fun to talk and enjoy each other's friendship and conversation.

Because Linh Phuong and I were quick with needle and thread, we also strung small, two-inch pieces of bamboo together. Other families painted delicate scenes on the bamboo sticks. The result was a beautiful floor-to-ceiling bamboo curtain that was sold at the marketplace.

One neighbor taught me the art of embroidery. She learned it from a Soviet Union woman who had moved to Saigon. This neighbor started an embroidery business out of her home, and I became an expert in embroidering scenes on pillowcases, bedspreads, and canvas. Once the products were finished, we washed, packaged, and exported them to the Soviet Union.

I was determined to help my family earn money so that we could survive. I wanted to excel at the items I was making. I eagerly learned new skills because I hoped that it would make a difference.

I also wanted to prove to others that people who are differently abled are capable of succeeding.

We tried our hand at a bamboo basket business but found it was challenging and there wasn't a good return on our time and resources. My brother learned the silk-screening business and became masterful at placing images on T-shirts and packaging. He also sold items for home renovation projects: bricks, Sheetrock, and tile.

Each alley community made fireworks to sell. Communities competed aggressively to see who could make the best fireworks. We utilized the assembly-line approach for firework production. Our family made the firework tube shells by rolling each sheet of paper until it was very tight. We created a hole in the middle of the tube and then passed it to the next family, who inserted the gunpowder into the hole. Another family group inserted the wicks. The last family in the assembly line sealed the bottom of the firecracker with cement and attached it to a base.

Every year before Tet, each family made fireworks that were judged in a competition. It was exciting to plan how to make the best fireworks to celebrate our Lunar New Year's Eve and New Year's Day. In preparation, my brother found a piece of plywood I sat on as he rolled the firecracker shells. He then inserted the wicks and cemented the base to the firecracker. We made three strings of firecrackers and three extra strings for backup: one for New Year's Eve, one for New Year's Day, and the final one for the day after New Year's.

The competition was judged by a group of people experienced in making firecrackers. After inspecting the firecracker design and creativity and evaluating the size and shape of the paper once the firework exploded, we won first prize one year. The prize was the pride we carried with us for years and the memories we had making the fireworks.

During Tet, floors were not supposed to be swept for three days, or good luck could be swept away for the upcoming year. During this time of year, I used to get very dirty because I moved along on the ground and floors were dirty from creating and shooting off fireworks, as well as messy from the food preparations. I didn't mind the litter on the floor because Tet was such a special time of year.

Our life was austere, and our belongings were meager, but we considered ourselves lucky because we had each other.

CHAPTER 5

Stairway to School

"Mom, I really want to go to school!"

After Mom returned from farming government land, the topic of school was a continual discussion between me and Mom. I watched forlornly every day as my brother and sister headed to school. I didn't understand why I couldn't go too. I constantly pleaded with Mom to let me attend school so that I could learn and be with other kids my own age.

As I got older, I changed the way I moved around on the floor. Rather than crawling, I sat in a squatting position. I hooked my right arm around my right knee and moved my right foot about four inches forward; then I repeated the process with my left arm hooked around my left knee. It was a slow, laborious, awkward process, but it was better than crawling. I learned to ignore the stares and whispered comments and kept my head held high when I was out in public.

Mom was concerned about how other kids would treat me. In Vietnam, handicapped children and adults were treated like discarded trash and useless human beings. There weren't any programs or resources from the government to help them. I often saw disabled people begging for money while sitting near the street;

either they didn't have relatives to take care of them or they had been abandoned by their families. It felt like society didn't value people who were differently abled.

I was relentless, so finally Mom agreed that I could go to kindergarten. I was eight years old at the time and much older than the other children in the class. After a few months, I moved from kindergarten to first grade.

Miss Lanh, my first-grade teacher, was very understanding, and she encouraged me to take the test to move to second grade. I can still clearly see Miss Lanh in her beautiful traditional Vietnamese clothing, with a form-fitting silk tunic over pants, called *ao dai*, that she wore every day to school. The Communist government did not want anyone wearing an *ao dai* because it was a reminder of the previous South Vietnamese government era. Miss Lanh was someone who stood up for what she believed was right. I admired her and wanted to grow up to be just like her.

Miss Lanh helped me learn after school so that I would be well prepared to take the test to go into second grade. She was someone who believed in me and wanted to see me continue to learn and stay in school. I passed the test and moved to second grade quickly, where I was with students my same age.

Mom worried about how other children would treat me. When I started attending school, some kids stared, snickered, and made fun of me, but most were nice, and I made some friends. However, one boy started picking on me. He would grab my backpack and throw it. Then I would have to retrieve it with my slow, awkward squatting movement by wrapping one arm around each leg and moving one foot at a time about four inches.

At first, when this boy threw my backpack, I cried. The male teacher didn't seem to notice or care, even when I sobbed loudly. Then I became angry when it happened. I started thinking of ways to stop this boy from tormenting me.

Before the Communists captured Saigon, girls wore a white *ao dai* to school, and boys wore black pants with a white shirt. When the Communists seized control, they required girls and boys to wear the same school uniform—black pants and a white shirt. Clothing was an expensive luxury, so most children only had one or two school uniforms. I had two school uniforms. Each night, Mom washed the uniform I had worn that day and strung the pants and shirt on a wire in the yard to dry.

We didn't have enough money to buy pencils or pens, so we made bottles of ink at home with a purple fruit, *hat mong toi*. It was a fruit like pokeberry that was used to dye fabric. After boiling and mashing the fruit, we poured the liquid into a bottle. We used a dip pen as our writing tool. We placed the dip pen in the bottle of ink and then wrote a few letters, let the paper dry, and then dipped the pen again into the ink. We had to be careful writing to make sure that the fruit ink didn't absorb onto the page underneath the page we were writing on, or our hands were slapped with rulers by the teacher.

One night, I decided to make two bottles of ink. The next day at school, when the boy grabbed my backpack, I decided that enough was enough. I opened the extra bottle of ink and hurled it at his white shirt. Instantly, his shirt transformed into a bold, purple burst of color. He started crying and wailed, "I only have one shirt for school."

The teacher roughly grabbed me by my shirt collar and dragged me to the front of the classroom.

He asked, "Which hand did you use to throw the bottle of ink?"

I told a small lie because I didn't want the teacher to hurt the hand I wrote with. "I used my left hand."

"Open your left palm right now."

The teacher grabbed his large wooden ruler and raised it way above his head. He paused for dramatic effect and then aggressively hit me on my open palm. Pain seared from my hand to my shoulder, but I was determined not to cry. He continued to thrash my palm with forty lashes. My palm was bright red and swollen with blisters. I remained stoic. I did not want to give him the satisfaction that he had hurt me.

The lashes on my palm were one of my most painful images of a victim being victimized a second time. When I cried each time the boy threw my backpack, my teacher ignored me, and I felt invisible. When I chose to do something about the bad behavior, I was victimized again. It was a weird dynamic that I have since seen repeatedly.

After that incident, the principal asked Mom to come to his office. He lectured her about my disobedience. He was demeaning and degrading to Mom and said that she didn't know how to educate or discipline her children. He insulted her by saying that the reason she couldn't educate her children was because she didn't have a husband.

When we got home, Mom's neck and face got bright red as she furiously screamed at me. Her words wounded me to the core. "You don't love me. You don't know how hard I work to try to put food on the table, and the thanks I get from you is trouble at school." I got scared when I saw how angry Mom was at me. I cried and promised Mom it would never happen again.

In addition to being picked on and whispered about at school, the restroom situation was challenging for me. Squatting toilets were the norm in Vietnam. A squatting toilet was basically a hole in the ground with porcelain around it. There was usually a water hose or a bucket nearby to wash urine and feces farther into the hole.

Because of the way I had to walk in a squatting motion with one arm wrapped around each knee to propel each foot forward a short distance, I was close to the squalor. The school squatting toilet areas were often unsanitary, slippery, and oozing with dreadful odors. I simply chose to "hold it" and did not use the restroom facilities during the school day.

Thankfully, Linh Phuong helped me at school by carrying me on her back up the flight of stairs. During lunchtime and recess, she left her friends and came to see me. When Linh Phuong started middle school, we were no longer at the same school. My fourth and fifth grade classes were on the third level. Initially, Mom carried me on her back, piggyback style, so that I could get to my classrooms.

After a while, I no longer wanted Mom to carry me up the stairs, so I begged her to let me climb the stairs by myself. I wanted to be independent. My friends helped me by carrying my backpack up the stairs for me. I pulled myself up each stair by grabbing the lower part of the railing with my arms and propelling myself slowly up each step.

Coming down the stairs was a whole 'nother story. The stairs were made of granite that was smooth and cool to the touch, especially when the weather was hot. On both sides of the stairs, there were large, wide banisters made of granite. In my mind, the banister was a huge slide that enabled me to get down the three levels of stairs quickly. It was also fun and fast!

It was so much fun that my friends also got down the stairs that way. It was our treat to ourselves once school was out. One day, the principal rounded the corner near the stairs as I was sliding fast and furiously down the smooth banister. The principal asked me to come into his office.

The principal asked me why I was sliding down the banister; I told him that it was much easier for me to slide than to maneuver laboriously down three flights of stairs in a squatting position. The principal instructed me not to slide down the banister anymore because other kids were doing it and it was dangerous. He didn't offer a different solution on how I could come down three long, steep flights of stairs.

I devised my own solution. My friends acted as lookout sentries to ensure that the principal wasn't around before I slid down the banister. Then I watched for the principal while my friends slid down the banister. We did not want to give up our awesome slide.

While I was in elementary and middle school, there was one other disabled student. He was a few years older than me, and he walked with crutches. He had polio in his left leg, which dangled limply as he maneuvered on his right leg. He stood upright with crutches and moved more fluidly than I did. However, he dropped out of school due to the unrelenting teasing he received.

My fifth-grade teacher, Mr. Nguyen, was a great role model and a huge influence on my life. He recognized leadership qualities in me and asked if I wanted to be involved in extracurricular activities at school. I eagerly replied, "Yes."

During lunch periods and recesses, I sat and watched other children playing and having fun. I often felt lonely and left out during these times. Doing extracurricular activities kept me engaged and active.

Mr. Nguyen mentioned that he had noticed I was good at layout, and he asked if I would create the annual school yearbook, *bich bao*. I worked excitedly on this project and spent hours perfecting the layout with articles written by my schoolmates and pictures of our activities throughout the year. I spent painstaking detail creating decorated pages and placing photos in the perfect position. I added cutout flowers and decorative borders to liven the pages.

All of the students and Mr. Nguyen complimented me on the school yearbook. I felt included, appreciated, and valued. I was asked to create the school yearbook each year for the next several years: fifth, sixth, seventh, and eighth grades. This experience taught me to autograph my work with excellence.

Every classroom designated one student as the class lead, *lop truong*, for each school year. The class lead asked the class to rise and greet the teacher when the teacher entered the room in the morning. The class lead was also responsible for roll call, communicating homework assignments, helping classmates with homework, and organizing class activities. I was selected to be the co–class lead of our fifth-grade class along with another student.

My experiences at school and during incredibly challenging situations taught me several powerful life lessons. I have used these learnings throughout my life and continue to practice them as I look toward the future. These three core values are the intangibles I pack in my daily backpack.

The first lesson is the power of hope. Hope had gotten me through my bleakest moments: war, the death of my dad, famine, and stark poverty. I knew that hope would get me through any difficulties in the future. I believed that if I had hope, I had every-thing. If I lost hope, I feared that I wouldn't have the will to survive. I used hope to imagine a better life for me and my family. Hope was a small voice inside my head whispering *maybe* when others around me were focused on negative thoughts.

The second lesson I learned is determination. Determination required that I live my life purposefully. Education was what I focused on. I believed that completing school could open doors for the future that I was imagining. I became resolute and steadfast in pursuing my goal of being able to go to college. What helped me remain determined was always having a positive attitude. I truly believe that positive attitudes create positive outcomes.

The third life lesson is personal reinvention. I have had to reinvent myself multiple times when I faced what seemed like insurmountable obstacles: developing polio, losing my dad, and living under Communist rule. It wasn't easy, but I can't imagine what my life would have been like if I didn't continually challenge myself and learn new skills. Learning can never be taken away; it is a treasure that travels with me wherever I may go. My teacher shared a quote with me: "If you are not willing to learn, no one can help you. If you are determined to learn, no one can stop you." I hope that my focus on constantly reinventing myself by always learning new things makes me unstoppable.

Little did I know that these three magnificent lessons would carry me through some tumultuous, life-altering experiences.

CHAPTER 6

Rising from the Dead

One day in 1980, five years after the fall of Saigon, I was at home while Mom and Linh Phuong were at the marketplace selling rice and feather dusters. I heard a loud and urgent knock at the door. When I opened the door, I was excited to see Uncle Xuan. Next to him stood an elderly man I had not seen before.

My uncle excitedly burst into the room and scooped me up in his arms. "Congratulations, Thu Hang, your dad is alive!"

I was confused. I didn't understand what he was saying. We had been told five years ago that Dad died in a helicopter crash. His belongings had been delivered to us. We'd held his Mass and funeral service. For the past five years, we had honored Dad during Tet. I looked over at Dad's photo on the family altar. I wanted to believe my uncle, but I wasn't sure.

Uncle Xuan started talking so fast that I could barely keep up with what he was saying. "This is Minh's father. Your dad is a close friend with Minh in San Antonio. Your dad has been searching for you for the past five years, and now he has found you. Where is your mom?"

I told him that Mom was at the Cho Xom Moi marketplace. I went outside and asked our neighbor to run fast to the market and tell my mom and sister to come home immediately. "Tell them there is news that my dad is alive!"

While we were waiting for my mom and sister, Uncle Xuan told me that Dad was living in San Antonio in the United States. I was ten years old and not knowledgeable about the world outside of our alley. I didn't know what the words *San Antonio* and *United States* meant. Was Dad close by or far away?

My mom and sister came bursting into the house, out of breath from running so hard and fast from the marketplace. "What is the news about Chinh?" Mom gasped.

Minh's father said, "I have great news! Chinh is alive and living in the United States. He is a friend of my son, and he has been trying to find you and your children for the past five years. Chinh has sent so many letters to you!"

"I want to believe you so badly, but we were told that he died in a helicopter crash. His friend brought Chinh's suitcase with his belongings to us."

Mom walked to the family altar in the living room and put her hand on the photo of Dad that had been placed there five years ago. "We held a funeral service for him five years ago and mourned his passing in Vietnamese tradition."

Words continued to tumble out. "How can we believe what you are saying? How do you have proof that my Chinh is still alive?"

Minh's father put his arm around Mom and gently had her sit down. He pulled out Chinh's letter and photo and placed them on her lap. She immediately noticed Chinh's handwriting and started sobbing.

At this point, my brother walked into the house, unaware of the enormity of the news that we had just received. I told him that Dad had been found and that he was alive. Quang Phuong, Linh Phuong, and I started jumping up and down, hugging each other, laughing, and crying.

Minh's father asked if we had a photo he could take back to Dad as proof that his family had been found. He specifically asked for a photo of the family before 1975 so that Dad could confirm it was his family. Dad had heard about unethical people claiming to look for families, as well as saying families had been found—only to be duped.

Mom's face dropped, and her shoulders slumped. She told Minh's father that when the Communists took over, they insisted that all citizens burn anything about South Vietnam, including all photos, documents, books, and videos.

"Mom. Mom. Mom. I have some photos of us as a family from before the war!" I said excitedly.

Mom shook her head sadly. "We burned all of our photos for fear of being punished."

"Mom, I couldn't bear to part with some of our family photos, so I buried a few photos in a tin can."

The room went silent. Everyone looked at me with their mouths wide open.

"You did *what*?" Mom asked in disbelief.

"I wanted to keep memories of our wonderful life as a family. When you were burning our photos, I kept a few photos hidden in a tin can. Later, I buried the tin can behind the kitchen cabinet near the entrance to the *ham*."

"Are they still buried in the *ham*?" Mom asked incredulously.

"Actually, I retrieved them from the *ham* after you returned from farming in Trang Bom, and I've kept them in the same tin can. I put the tin can inside of Dad's dark-blue suitcase. I'll go get it."

Dad's dark-blue suitcase was my personal reminder of our previous life and how happy we had been as a family. I kept his suitcase in the bottom drawer of my dresser. When no one was looking, I often took it out and lovingly looked at his belongings. I stared at the photo of him at the air traffic control tower and imagined the times he'd held me in his arms.

I retrieved Dad's valise and pulled out the tin can that held several family photos. We decided to give Minh's father two photos. One photo was taken in 1972 with two nuns from our church. Mom is holding me; Linh Phuong and Quang Phuong are standing next to Mom. We also wanted to give Dad a current photo of our family. We chose a photo with Quang Phuong looking handsome and confident while wearing Dad's military hat, Mom in her favorite floral *ao dai*, and Linh Phuong and me.

This was one of the happiest days of my life.

PART II

CHINH

CHAPTER 7

Vietnam Vortex

As Thuhang's father, April 30, 1975, was the darkest day of my life. I lost my family that day. While fleeing for my life, I didn't know that I wouldn't see them again for almost fifteen years. Each time I share my story, darkness brings terrible nightmares, and I relive intensely painful memories.

Historical context helps shape an understanding of my journey. Vietnam is an S-shaped country with over one thousand miles of coast. Vietnam borders the Gulf of Thailand, the Gulf of Tonkin, and the South China Sea. China is across our northern border, and Cambodia and Laos are our western neighbors. Our geographic location seems to invite war.

Vietnam has been ruled by several different countries. Long ago, many different Chinese dynasties ruled Vietnam, including the Ming Empire. The French ruled for almost a century, followed by a brief Japanese occupation of Vietnam during World War II. Ho Chi Minh and his Viet Minh Communist troops took advantage of the abrupt end of French rule and the retreat of the Japanese from World War II with several strategic attacks. Japan's surrender in September 1945 raised the question about who would rule Vietnam.

The First Indochina War, also known as the Franco–Viet Minh War, immediately commenced in September 1945 after World War II ended. This was a unique episode in global history because the Soviet Union, China, and the United States viewed Vietnam as critical to their goals of prevailing in a global struggle; all three countries intervened in Vietnam.

The Cold War began after World War II ended and changed everything. The world split into two blocs, the United States and the Soviet Union. Vietnam was a key part of the worldwide struggle between democracy and communism.

Ho Chi Minh, whose name means "He Who Enlightens," had a two-prong approach capable of influencing many Vietnamese. During the First Indochina War and the Vietnam War, Ho Chi Minh fought for communism as well as for Vietnam's independence. He continually reiterated his nationalist approach by stating that Vietnam was not anyone's lapdog. He struck a chord with citizens regarding his zeal for independence. He asserted that Vietnam should be *con rong chau tien*, a sovereign nation.[2]

Dividing Vietnam into two halves as part of the Geneva Accords in 1954 was similar to the division of Korea after the Korean War ended in July 1953. Vietnamese citizens had three hundred days to migrate to the North or the South. It is estimated that between one to two million people moved from the North to the South.[3] However, thousands of Southerners who had fought in the Communist Viet Minh forces stayed in the South and were hostile to the new regime.[4]

I was born in Son Tay, twenty-two miles west of Hanoi and in the shadow of the steep peaks of the majestic Ba Vi mountain range. When I was a child, my parents were separated for ten years due to the First Indochina War. My dad served in the military, and we rarely saw him. When the war ended, we moved to South Vietnam. I was excited we were going to be a family again, but my happiness was short lived. My father was angry, with violent outbursts that included striking me or my mom.

In 1961, when I was seventeen years old, my baby brother, Dinh, was born. He brought joy into our lives with his broad smile and giggling sounds. My mom's health deteriorated after his birth, and she passed away when he was six months old. My mom had been my best friend; she encouraged me and believed in me. She was my mooring, my anchor; I felt adrift without her.

I knew that I had to be strong and take care of Dinh. My responsibilities quadrupled overnight. In addition to attending school, I took care of our pigs, located firewood in the jungle, prepared our meals, took care of my brother, and earned an income.

As I became a young man, the political and military climate continued to change. Fighting between the North and South intensified. South Vietnam's President Ngo Dinh Diem was heavily criticized due to widespread corruption. Diem's brother, Ngo Dinh Nhu, ran the military and secret police force with unbridled aggression. Buddhist protests resulted in tragic deaths, self-immolations, and public outrage, which paved the path for a coup d'etat.

I joined the South Vietnam Air Force on November 4, 1963, two days after the assassinations of South Vietnam President Diem and his brother, Nhu. US President John F. Kennedy was assassinated three weeks later in Dallas, Texas.

South Vietnam experienced six different leadership regimes between 1963 and 1965. These short-lived military-oriented governments created instability and constant change for citizens. Throughout these leadership changes, Nguyen Van Thieu moved up the ranks. Thieu became the leader of South Vietnam in 1965 and remained in power for ten years until two days before the fall of Saigon.

Fast-forward to January 1973, when the United States ended their involvement in the Vietnam War. There was a ceasefire agreement on paper, but neither the North nor the South stopped fighting. The Ho Chi Minh Trail along the Laos and Cambodian borders operated as a superhighway for the Viet Cong to supply men and weapons.

The course of history changed on August 9, 1974, when US President Richard Nixon resigned. With Nixon's downfall, the Communists created a two-year strategy to conquer South Vietnam. To test the new American president, Gerald Ford, the Viet Cong launched a major attack on December 13, 1974, at Phuoc Long, just fifty miles northeast of Saigon. There was no response from US President Ford or the US military when Phuoc Long fell to the Communists.

Against this backdrop of American disinterest, Communist forces began their singular focus on conquering South Vietnam. The Central Highlands were attacked in March 1975. The battle at Ban Me Thuot in the Central Highlands was a critical turning point of the war. South Vietnam President Thieu made a grave error and ordered all troops southward.

The large city of Hue was next. Hue was symbolic because of the huge massacre during the Tet Offensive in 1968. During the longest and bloodiest battle of the war, Communist forces executed two thousand eight hundred Hue civilians, including burying people alive.

Hue fell easily on March 24, 1975. Thousands of civilians fled Hue on foot with minimal belongings and headed south to Da Nang on Highway 1, aptly nicknamed the "Street Without Joy." The Viet Cong forces were right behind them.

Da Nang had over one million civilians seeking refuge when the Communists showed up. It was utter chaos. At the port, civilians were throwing their babies onto boats with the hope of a better life even if it meant their child wasn't with them. Sometimes, the baby wouldn't make it to the boat and fell in the water.[5]

Da Nang quickly fell on March 28. It was frightful to hear of the rapid onslaught of the enemy during the daily war updates that I received. My comrades and I were aghast with news about the large desertion rates of South Vietnamese soldiers.

During March and April 1975, there were many rumors about our country's future and President Thieu. There was speculation about potential coups. Pressure mounted for Thieu to resign so that a new regime could improve our military strategy or negotiate with the Communists.

One of the major rumors was whether South Vietnam would shrink in size. There was a strong belief that Vietnam would still be split in two, but South Vietnam would start at Saigon or possibly at Can Tho. We knew that the provinces north of Saigon had fallen, but we hadn't seen much fighting south of Saigon for almost two years.

That changed on April 14, 1975, when Can Tho was heavily shelled. The same week, Communist forces attacked Xuan Loc, the last major city north of Saigon. Intense fighting occurred for twelve days at Xuan Loc as both sides fought ferociously to win. On April 20, under cover of heavy rain, South Vietnam forces withdrew. Saigon was in sight for the Communists.

The week before Communist forces arrived in Saigon, daily life had some semblance of normalcy. Shops were open for business, and schools remained open. US Ambassador Graham Martin had not started a formal evacuation prior to Communist troops arriving in Saigon because he hoped that the United States would provide last-minute aid, and he did not want to create chaos and panic. Ambassador Martin's foster son had been killed in battle in Vietnam, and Martin felt a close connection to the people of South Vietnam.[6]

On April 29, 1975, I received reports that Saigon had been hit with rockets, and Tan Son Nhat Airport was inoperable. I was worried about my family because our home was close to the airport. I said many prayers, hoping God would hear me and save them. It felt like Vietnam was in a hellish vortex.

We were instructed to provide many of our helicopters from Can Tho for the urgent evacuations occurring on the embassy grounds in Saigon. Later, I found out that some of our pilots had flown themselves and family members out to the South China Sea rather than participate in the embassy evacuation. It was sheer chaos; panic was palpable.

On the morning of April 30, 1975, President Minh announced the unconditional surrender of South Vietnam. The war was over. It was somewhat ironic because the following day was International Labor Day, a public holiday in Vietnam. I remained at the air base, debating the best course of action to take while continuing to work.

I called home in the late afternoon. My brother Dinh answered. I didn't have much time, so I told him that I was going to drive a car from the Can Tho Air Base to our home in Saigon, gather Dinh and my family, and then drive to the Tan Son Nhat Airport. I asked Dinh to speak quietly with Lieu and have her pack one suitcase for our journey out of the country.

I was confident that my military and airport experience would help me find a way out of the country for all of us. I knew the Tan Son Nhat Airport like the back of my hand, and I knew where all of the helicopters, airplanes, and potential escape routes existed.

Although I told Dinh that I was ready to leave the country with my family, I was deeply conflicted. I continued to debate about whether we should stay or go. South Vietnam was our home, and we had deep roots and connections to our beloved country. I wasn't sure what the future would hold if we escaped to another country.

The night before, a senior-ranking military official had fled the country and told me that his car was available to use. It was late afternoon on April 30 when I packed my suitcase to prepare to leave. I was headed to his car to go get my family when a colonel stopped me and asked, "What the hell are you still doing here?"

Because I was conflicted about staying or leaving and because I wasn't sure how honest I could be, I replied, "I'm not planning on leaving. My family needs me, and I want to stay with them. I'm very worried about my daughter Thu Hang."

The colonel stopped dead in his tracks and looked directly into my eyes. "You can't stay here. I know that your family is very important to you. If you stay here, you will be killed, and you'll never see your family. You must leave the country immediately."

I asked the colonel why he was remaining behind; he replied that he was going to stay and work with the new government. I shook his hand and said, "Thank you, sir," and then I grabbed my suitcase and sprinted for the airport tarmac.

Near the runway, there were four or five remaining helicopters. I knew that those helicopters were ones with mechanical problems and little fuel. Throngs of people were trying to climb aboard the few remaining choppers. Major Phan saw me and said, "Hey, Chinh, I know that there is one more helicopter at the Vietnamese Army IV Corp headquarters . . . Let's fly one of these birds over there. Follow me!"

We ran to one of the helicopters, and, although I was not a copilot, I sat in the copilot's seat. The gas gauge indicated that we only had enough fuel for ten to fifteen minutes of flight. Military and airport personnel and civilians began climbing aboard and swarming the helicopter. We had over twenty-five people on board—typically, we carry seven to ten people on a helicopter. I had to brandish my gun at others who wanted to climb aboard. I knew that we could potentially crash or not be able to lift off if our load was too heavy.

We flew a helicopter with wing number 790 from Can Tho Air Base to the Vietnamese Army IV Corp headquarters. There we boarded a different helicopter—it had belonged to General Hoang's second lieutenant. Hoang's officer had evacuated the night before. I signaled to a man named Captain Thanh to start the engine. We took off about 5:30 p.m. and landed at Con Son Island around 6:00 p.m. Con Son Island is a Vietnamese island directly south of Vietnam.

When we transferred helicopters at the Vietnamese Army IV Corp headquarters, I accidentally left my suitcase on the first helicopter with wing number 790. Chaos had erupted, and there were throngs of military personnel and civilians trying to escape. My focus was on flying toward freedom; I wasn't focused on keeping track of my belongings.

Many years later, I learned that the original helicopter, number 790, that we had flown to army headquarters was flown back to Can Tho Air Base. The helicopter refueled and attempted to take off. Unfortunately, the helicopter was overloaded with too many people, and it crashed shortly after takeoff. My suitcase, along with other people's belongings, bounced out of the helicopter upon impact.

As we were flying our helicopter toward Con Son Island, it was eerie because there weren't any air traffic control communications. It was deathly silent. As we looked out our window, we saw helicopters crashing into the sea. We weren't sure if the pilots had run out of fuel, had experienced mechanical problems, or were deliberately crashing.

We saw swarms of aircraft carriers in the South China Sea; many of them were unmarked. We didn't know which ships were friendly allies and which ones were foes. We watched in stunned disbelief as helicopters were pushed into the sea from the landing pads on aircraft carriers. Then we realized that those actions were necessary to make space for other helicopters to land on the carriers.

When the helicopter landed at Con Son Island, it was raining hard. The rain was so thick and heavy, it felt like heaven was crying. I sprinted in the torrential rain to the civilian ship docked at Con Son Island. I saw many other high-ranking South Vietnamese military officers on the ship. They did not know the nationality of the ship. When I asked questions about the ship's nationality, I was only told, "If you want to stay with us, we will take care of you. If you don't want to stay with us, you are welcome to leave." I decided to stay.

I had not eaten any food all day, and I was famished. I heard a young voice say, "Hey, Uncle, would you like some rice?" It was a four-year-old boy, and he was tapping my leg as he asked me the question. He handed me a huge, clear-plastic bag filled with rice that was topped with Peking duck. I quickly asked the four or five military officers standing by me if they wanted some rice and duck. All of us were starving. I grabbed a handful of rice, placed it in each of their outstretched hands, and then added some of the duck on top.

About fifteen minutes later, I felt a tapping on my leg again. The young boy asked if I would like dessert. He eagerly gave me *che dau*, a bean-pudding dessert garnished with coconut crème, and I shared it with the others. I searched for this young boy so that I could thank him, but I never saw him again.

While standing on the deck of the civilian ship, I noticed that the air was almost completely black. There were swarms of helicopters of all sizes; it looked like an invasion of locusts. Several helicopter pilots were trying to determine what to do. Pilots were trying to locate the US Seventh Fleet, which was somewhere in the South China Sea. I knew the radio frequency the US Navy used and the approximate coordinates where the fleet was stationed. I got on the ship's radio and communicated the frequency information to the helicopter pilots.

Thirty minutes after boarding the civilian ship docked at Con Son Island, the ship began moving. I wasn't sure where we were going, but I hoped that it was toward safety and freedom. An hour later, we pulled alongside a ship that was part of the US Seventh Fleet.

There were two military policemen (MPs) coordinating the arrival of all refugees onto the US ship. All ammunition, weapons, grenades, and sharp objects had to be thrown into the sea before boarding. Any military clothing had to also be thrown into the sea. I was wearing a friend's pilot jacket at the time, so I took it off and tossed it.

The MPs noticed that I spoke English and Vietnamese, so they asked if I could help them interpret and communicate with those boarding the ship. I agreed to help; I answered many questions and comforted distressed people. The MPs searched luggage and personal belongings while refugees waited in another area.

In one suitcase, the MP found several heavy metal bars the size of small bricks. He turned one of the black bricks over in his hands several times as he evaluated it. He ended up tossing the bricks in the ocean because he wasn't sure what they were. When the elderly man retrieved his suitcase after it had been searched, he looked concerned.

I asked him if there was a problem. The man replied that his black bars were missing from his suitcase. I asked him what the black bars were, and he indicated that they were bars of gold he had painted black as a disguise. I told the man that his black bricks had been thrown into the sea. He fainted when I told him that his entire life savings had been deposited into the water.

There were at least four thousand people on the US Navy ship. Although there wasn't enough food and water, no one complained. Each person received half a cup of rice each day and one Dixie paper cup of water. Everyone seemed deep in thought about their unknown futures.

We arrived in the Philippines at the US Naval Base in Subic Bay after several days at sea. There were many US ships helping refugees, including the USS *Kirk*, the USS *Mobile*, the USS *Tuscaloosa*, the USS *Barbour County*, and several others. The US Seventh Fleet closely watched South Vietnamese traveling on their own vessels. If any of the South Vietnamese boats or people on the boats started experiencing trouble, the US captains quickly provided assistance.

As our ship approached the Philippine port, the ship captain received word that the presence of South Vietnamese boats at a Philippine port was problematic because Ferdinand Marcos, president of the Philippines, was one of the first world leaders to recognize the new Communist government in Vietnam. President Marcos felt that South Vietnamese boats now belonged to the victorious regime.

A thoughtful and diplomatic solution was quickly presented by South Vietnam Captain Do and agreed upon. The South Vietnamese ships were treated as a loan from the United States during the war. Now that the war was over, a ceremonial transfer of power from the South Vietnamese ships back to the United States would enable all vessels flying an American flag to enter the Philippine harbor.[7]

There was an immediate search to find extra American flags to give to the South Vietnamese boats for the ceremonial transfer of power. As the South Vietnamese flag was lowered from each vessel, thousands and thousands of people began singing the South Vietnam national anthem, *"Tieng Goi Cong Dan."* As the singing echoed across the waves, the sounds of sobs intertwined with the lyrics. I held my hand over my broken heart and sang a choked farewell to my country and my family.

CHAPTER 8

Enlisting the Aid of Friends

As our boat docked in the Philippines, my heart was heavy. I was racked with doubt about leaving South Vietnam and my family. To calm myself down, I focused on the possibilities for the future and imagined being together again.

Upon exiting the boat, US Navy personnel directed people to different lines. I talked with several American naval officers about my work experience as an air traffic controller. They advised me to wait and go with a separate group of refugees to a different meeting area. I met with a captain who told me that I would be taken to Andersen Air Force Base in Guam.

The next day, I boarded an airplane headed to Guam, a US territory. Freedom was in sight, but my family and my heart were left behind.

After spending several weeks in Guam, I flew to Ft. Smith, Arkansas, and was taken to the refugee camp at the Fort Chaffee military base on May 20, 1975. There were many Vietnamese refugees on the base. Later, it was reported that over fifty-one thousand Vietnamese refugees stayed at Fort Chaffee between 1975 and 1976.[8]

The base was well organized with two-story wooden houses spaced closely together in an orderly fashion. There were social activities, church services, and educational programs for children and adults. Despite all of the amenities, I felt out of place and missed my family badly.

As additional South Vietnamese military officers and servicemen arrived at Fort Chaffee, I heard information about some of the military officers who had remained in South Vietnam. General Pham Van Phu had served as the chief of staff of the Special Forces and commander of II Corp Tactical Zone in Pleiku. He was the commander at the battle of Ban Me Thuot. Phu committed suicide on April 30 when Saigon fell. Several other military leaders also killed themselves.

I tried many times to locate my family or find information about them. I sent letters on a regular basis but never heard back. Every time I met a refugee from the Saigon area, I asked if they knew anything about my family, but each time the answer was no.

In early July 1975, I was told that a sponsor had chosen me, and I would be moving to South Dakota. Sponsors were required to provide housing and employment. My sponsor was a wealthy and powerful woman named Kay Riordan. She was the owner of Mountain Company, the only restaurant and gift shop at Mount Rushmore in Keystone, South Dakota. Kay was close personal friends with South Dakota US Senator George McGovern and his wife, Eleanor.

I flew to Rapid City, South Dakota, and a young couple, Joe and Linda, met me at the airport. They asked if I had any luggage; I replied no. I only had the clothes on my back. The drive from Rapid City to Keystone took about a half hour. I learned that Joe and Linda were engaged to be married, and they both worked at Mountain Company.

When we arrived in Keystone, it was late at night. I was shown where I would be staying. It was a room the size of a large closet. There were two bunk beds. Three guys were sleeping in the bunks, so I lay down on the empty bottom bunk and quickly fell asleep.

Several hours later, at 4:00 a.m., there was an urgent knock on the door. I woke up disoriented; I didn't know where I was. There was a huge, imposing bear of a man standing at the door. He was the chef, and he informed me that it was "time to go to work, boy." I quickly washed my face and followed him.

Inside the kitchen, he asked me if I knew how to break eggs and cook them. I answered, "No"; he showed me how to break one egg at a time in both hands. The first day, I cooked over four thousand eggs for the tourists lined up at the only restaurant at Mount Rushmore. I quickly learned to make eggs scrambled, poached, fried, over easy, and sunny-side up. Later in the day, I received a name badge indicating that I was the cook for Dining Facility E. Within a few days, I mastered breaking four eggs at a time in each hand.

On the second day of work, Kay informed me that I would be taking my driver's license test at the end of the week. She handed me the South Dakota Driver's Handbook and told me to study. I cooked for eight to ten hours each day and studied at night. On Friday, Kay took me to the Department of Motor Vehicles (DMV) for my driver's license. I passed the written test and was asked to take the driving test.

Kay drove a brand-new 1976 Silver Lake Cutlass; as I entered the car with the man from the DMV, he commented on the gorgeous car. I had owned and driven cars in Vietnam, so I wasn't nervous. I asked the man from the DMV where he wanted me to drive, and he said, "Wherever you want to go." The man had served a tour of duty in Vietnam, so we chatted amiably as I drove. I easily passed the driving test.

Being able to drive meant that on my days off, Mondays and Thursdays, I was expected to be Kay's personal chauffeur. I drove her to Rapid City for her regular routine of massages, facials, and nail appointments. I picked up her dry cleaning and waited in the car for her other appointments to be completed.

One day, while running errands for Kay, I drove to Ellsworth Air Force Base outside of Rapid City. I missed being an air traffic controller. I showed the MP at the air base gate my refugee papers and my Mountain Company work badge and asked if I could visit the base. I told the MP that I used to be an air traffic controller at the Saigon airport.

The MP made a call from his guard gate and waved me in. I spoke with an air traffic controller at Ellsworth who had served in Vietnam. He asked me if I wanted to hold the traffic controller's microphone. As much as I wanted to, I replied, "No." I knew that I had to return to my new life as a cook once I drove off of the base.

Mountain Company offered summer employment to hundreds of young men and women. My three bunkmates were college students. There was a separate dormitory building for young woman employees. During the night, women would crawl in our window and visit my bunkmates. We often had more than four people in our tiny room for the evening.

While I worked in South Dakota, some women would express an interest in me, but I felt like a dead person inside. I wasn't interested at all. I wanted to find my wife and family. One time, a young employee asked me to put suntan lotion on her back. When she lay down, she loosened the strings to her bikini top. After I rubbed suntan lotion on her back, she stood up and faced me naked without her bikini top. I didn't respond and just walked away. Later, she told many employees that I wasn't a man because I didn't get aroused seeing her naked.

I missed my family terribly and wanted to locate them. I was worried, particularly about Thu Hang. I knew that life in the Communist regime was incredibly difficult, and I wasn't sure how Thu Hang would survive. I continued to write letters to my family but never heard back.

Kay said that she was sponsoring a Vietnamese family who would be joining us at Keystone. It was a family of four: a mother, a father, and their two children. Rather than placing them in the dormitory living arrangements, they lived in Kay's five-story home. Their living quarters were very different from mine.

As summer turned to winter, the number of tourists declined. I learned how to make doughnuts, hot chocolate, and other food items. I worked in the gift store as business needs changed. I kept asking to learn other things. I wanted to continue to learn and improve my financial situation.

I wanted to get a college education and create opportunities for myself in the United States. I knew that this would not sit well with Kay. I felt that my life was in her hands since she was my sponsor. I spoke to a nun at the church for advice about speaking to Kay regarding my desire to attend college so that I could learn new skills. The nun said that she couldn't help me, and I shouldn't mention this idea to Kay. She reminded me that Kay was powerful and was close personal friends with Senator McGovern and his wife.

As the 1975 Christmas season approached, I became depressed. This was my first Christmas without my family. I missed them terribly, and I had no idea if they were still alive. I had a huge hole in my heart, and I didn't know how much longer I could live in this environment.

On Christmas Eve, Joe and Linda suggested that the Vietnamese family who lived in Kay's house and I go to town to choose a Christmas tree. After we selected a Christmas tree, we stopped at the liquor store for some whiskey and beer. When we returned, we decorated the tree in my tiny bunkhouse. While decorating the tree, we cried because we missed our lives and our loved ones in Vietnam. The liquor helped soothe our souls; soon we were laughing and having a good time. It reminded me of the expression "I laugh to keep from crying."

Kay knew that I missed my family terribly and wasn't happy. She wrote a letter to Senator George McGovern on December 26, 1975, because the senator was planning a trip to Vietnam in January 1976.

Imagine my surprise when Kay called Senator McGovern after sending the letter. Kay handed me the phone to speak with the senator. I asked him to try to contact my family only if he could absolutely bring them back to the United States with him. I said that I was worried that if he or someone on his team asked a person in the Communist regime to try to locate my family, it could mean disastrous consequences for my family. The Communists might assume that I, Chinh, must be a very important person, and it could mean death or harassment for my family.

Senator McGovern reassured me that he would not share my family's name or address; he would inquire in general terms about families left behind. He promised to send me a report about his trip. Senator McGovern sent me several reports after his trip to Vietnam. He was one of the few senators, at the time, who recommended abandoning the trade embargo against Vietnam and formally recognizing the new Vietnamese government.

Realizing that it might take some time before I had news about my family, I tried improving my financial situation. I approached Kay about purchasing a car. Kay asked how much I had saved and whether I could afford a car. My paycheck included deductions for room and food; after deductions, I barely made $100 every two weeks. I had saved about $1,100 to purchase a car.

During the middle of winter, Kay handed me an airline ticket to Las Vegas dated February 15, 1976. She said that her friend in Las Vegas wanted to sell her 1969 Volkswagen Hatchback. I had been in the United States about six months. This trip required me to fly to Las Vegas and drive myself back to South Dakota in the dead of winter. I jumped at the opportunity.

After arriving in Las Vegas, I stayed for several days, courtesy of Kay's friend, in a luxurious suite at the Four Queens Hotel. The suite was over one thousand square feet. I felt like the "king of the world." I played a few hands of blackjack and then knew that I needed to get on the road.

I prepared for my long road trip by packing some food, a can of gasoline, a blanket, and some warm clothes. I studied a map of the route ahead of time. The entire trip was over twelve hundred miles. I started on Highway 15, traveling from Vegas through scenic Utah. I was headed toward Salt Lake City. As I entered the state of Utah, it started to snow, and the temperature began dropping quickly.

The snow continued to fall heavily, and driving was treacherous. I continued to creep along, keeping my hands gripped tightly on the steering wheel. The windshield wipers grew heavy with crusted ice and snow. I rolled down my window, at times, to get cool air on the windshield so that I could see better.

I pulled over at a roadside restaurant. A rugged cowboy gruffly asked me, "What do you need, boy?"

I wearily replied, "I need some coffee." As he poured my coffee, he asked me where I was headed. I told him that I was driving to South Dakota, hoping to make it to Salt Lake City for the night. He told me that I couldn't drive anywhere; the roads were closed. I ordered some food and enjoyed the warmth of the coffee and a hot meal. I decided to ignore his advice about driving and got back in my car.

The next several hours of driving were incredibly slow. There wasn't anyone on the road, and conditions continued to deteriorate rapidly. I kept trying to see where the road was; I used the tall metal posts alongside the road as my guide. The snow was swirling viciously, which created a mesmerizing whiteout kaleidoscope.

I drove in eerie silence. There weren't any cars on the road. It was just me and my VW and a world of white wonderland. It was serene and peaceful. It was also dangerous, with tall drifts of snow as I slowly headed north on Highway 15 through Utah.

After several hours of driving, I thought I saw something moving alongside the road. Then I didn't see any movement. I wondered if I was hallucinating. My world consisted of a lot of white, swirling snow and some occasional bits of sun peeking from the grey clouds. But I saw movement again up ahead.

I started to slow down cautiously so that I could stop without sliding into or hitting the thing that was moving. I pumped my brakes in order to slowly come to a stop. I stared out of my window in amazement. There was a tall man standing beside the road. His beard was a frozen mass of ice.

I got out of my car and said, "Come here"; I opened the passenger door. The man did not move. I removed his backpack from his back and placed it in the trunk. He was still standing completely still, almost like a robot. I realized that he was frozen in place and couldn't move. He was unable to speak. I cranked up the heat in the car and helped him put one foot in front of the other until he was standing beside the car.

I helped the stranger sit down in the car with his legs extended outside the car door. He couldn't bend his legs to put them in the car. The car heater began to defrost his beard; the ice turned to rivers of water that flowed from his face to his coat and then plunked onto the car seat. I poured him a cup of coffee from my thermos, but he couldn't hold the cup. I gingerly placed the cup against his mouth and tilted it slightly. After fifteen minutes of warming up, I bent his knees and placed his legs inside the car.

When he was finally able to speak, his first words were, "Thank you. You saved my life." Later, the near-frozen hitchhiker said that he thought he had about thirty more minutes before he would have frozen to death. I felt that it was part of God's plan that I had continued driving on a closed interstate to find this man and rescue him. I dropped him off at his friend's home in Salt Lake City.

After dropping off my new friend, I turned onto Highway 80, headed east. With the road and weather conditions, I crept along cautiously for several hours. Around 11:00 p.m., I knew that I couldn't drive much farther.

Down the road, I saw a motel sign and carefully maneuvered my VW off of the highway into the parking lot. The motel sign wasn't lit, and I didn't see any other cars in the parking lot. I put on my jacket, hat, and gloves and slowly walked through the thigh-high mounds of snow to the front door of the motel. I knocked loudly on the door, but no one came.

It was almost midnight by now, so I cranked up the car and put the heat on full blast. Once the car was nice and toasty, I turned the car off. I bundled up in the blanket and kept my jacket, hat, and gloves on as I lay down to sleep in the backseat.

Early in the morning, I heard someone knocking on my car window. I opened the car door, and a man asked me what I was doing. I told him that I had been driving and had pulled over to stay at the motel, but no one was there. The man informed me that the motel was closed during the winter. He said that I was lucky to be alive and asked me where I was headed. I told him that I was driving to South Dakota. He replied, "You cannot go, son. The roads are closed. Come inside, and I'll make you some coffee."

The warmth of the coffee tingled as it made its way through my body. My limbs started to feel rejuvenated as I stretched. Call me hardheaded, but I felt that I needed to keep driving, so I got back on the road.

Once again, it was just me and my trusty car. The two of us took the road together very slowly. I missed having someone to talk with to make the time pass faster. The falling snow was gentler, and, occasionally, there were sporadic bursts of sun through the clouds.

Near Cheyenne, Wyoming, I turned north on Highway 25, which had just been reopened. I drove several hours until I picked up Highway 90, headed east into South Dakota. The drive from Las Vegas to Mount Rushmore takes twenty hours of nonstop driving during ideal weather conditions. My trip during the heart of winter took me over five days. When I arrived back at Mount Rushmore, no one could believe that I had driven that route by myself. They thought I was crazy.

During that long journey, I had plenty of time to think about my family and my future. I knew that I wanted to go to college and learn new skills. I was determined to speak with Kay about allowing me to attend school. I decided to speak to her after the busy summer season.

When I approached Kay with my request to go to college, she angrily pounded her fist on top of her desk and yelled, "You make good money here. You have a good job here. You don't need to go to college."

If I couldn't attend college, I was interested in obtaining an air traffic controller job since that was what I had done before coming to America. I submitted my request three different times to the United States Civil Service Commission. I received two letters worded almost identically on August 6, 1976, and August 19, 1976. The letters indicated that my application forms had been received and that the "processing of applications from noncitizens has been delayed, pending receipt of further instructions from our regional office."

I continued to apply for air traffic controller positions until I received the following response from the United States Civil Service Commission dated October 26, 1976. The letter stated:

We are returning your application for Federal employment. On September 2, 1976, President Ford signed Executive Order 11935 amending Civil Service Commission Rule VII to limit service positions to citizens unless excepted by the Civil Service Commission. Executive Order 11935 restores the longstanding restriction on alien employment in the Federal competitive service.

The letter continued for another two paragraphs and basically reiterated that I wasn't eligible for employment with the US government even though I had the skills and abilities and had spent the past decade helping the US military based in South Vietnam. While waiting on this last response, I decided to end my employment with Mountain Company.

I told Kay that I needed to leave to seek new work opportunities and attend college. I decided to move to San Antonio, Texas, because I had a friend there who had escaped South Vietnam when I did, and we had kept in touch. My road trip to San Antonio was uneventful compared to my Vegas to South Dakota adventure.

When I arrived in San Antonio, I rented an upstairs room from an elderly woman for $125 per month. I started looking for work and applied to attend San Antonio Community College. I needed a GED since I did not have documents indicating that I had graduated from high school in Vietnam. I studied diligently for two months and passed the GED. I started attending San Antonio Community College and focused on electrical engineering. While attending college, I found a job as a television repairman.

I kept trying to contact my family through letters, but I never heard back. One of my friends in San Antonio, Minh, mentioned that he had family in Vietnam and had contact with his family. I asked Minh if he could help find my family, and he eagerly said that he would do everything he could to help.

I drew a detailed map of my neighborhood in Saigon and indicated where my family had last been living, as well as where my wife's brother Truc had last been living. Minh mailed the map and instructions to his family in Vietnam and asked for their help.

Once the map and letter arrived in Vietnam, Minh's brother set out to find my family. As he was walking through Truc's neighborhood with the hand-drawn map, a Communist policeman approached him and asked him what he was doing. Unsatisfied with his explanation and suspicious of the map, the policeman arrested Minh's brother and placed him in jail. He languished in jail for about six months but was released once I sent several hundred dollars for bribery money.

Even though Minh's brother had been arrested, Minh was determined to find a way to locate my family. Whenever we met, he said, "We need to figure out a way to find your wife and children." Then an idea struck him: "I think my father should be the one to look for your family. An elderly man walking the streets looking for family members won't draw much attention."

I don't know if God was guiding me or not; since Minh's brother had been arrested in Truc's neighborhood, it seemed like I should try a different approach. I had no idea that Truc's home had been confiscated by the Communists and he had moved. This time, I drew a map to the home of Xuan, my other brother-in-law.

Lieu and I had rented a house next door to Xuan and his family for a short period of time in 1966 and 1967. I was hopeful that my wife's brother Xuan was still living in his home, particularly if my family had moved. I drew a new map that included the last-known locations of Xuan's home and my family's home. I included a hand-written letter to Lieu and a photo of myself in front of my home in San Antonio.

Mail from the United States to Vietnam was regularly opened and read by government officials, so I had to be careful with my correspondence. Mail often took six to twelve months to reach the intended recipient, if it arrived at all. I mailed the second map and letter and prayed every night that it would reach Minh's father.

After six months, my map arrived at Minh's father's home. Minh's father set out to find my family. His father lived in Nga Bay, which was closer to Xuan's home than my family's home, so he started searching for Xuan. My family's home was approximately six miles from Xuan's neighborhood. Minh's father conducted his search on a three-wheeled cyclo taxi.

It was another six months, a total of one year since I had drawn the second map, before Minh received news that my family had been found. When Minh knocked so loudly on my front door that the hinges vibrated, I knew that it had to be good news. I sobbed like a baby when I heard that my family was alive. Then I started hollering, "My family is alive! My family is alive!"

PART III

THUHANG

CHAPTER 9

Communication, Communism, and Cambodia

"My dad is alive! My dad is alive!" I repeated to myself each night as I said my prayers and tried to fall asleep. Once I knew that Dad was alive, I was anxious to be reunited with him—to touch him, hug him, and hear his voice.

The stark reality was that we lived under Communist rule, where association and correspondence with people from other countries, particularly the United States, could mean harassment, imprisonment, torture, and even death. We knew that our letters would likely be read by the Communist government before being sent to Dad. In our correspondence, we ensured that we never mentioned the government or their policies in a bad or harmful manner.

Postage was incredibly expensive, so Mom limited us to one page each when we sent letters to Dad. Mom had only gone to school until the second grade, so I became Mom's secretary. She asked me to write her letters to Dad. I felt like I was part of their private conversations. Mom gave Dad an overall view of our lives and how each of us was behaving. Sometimes, she mentioned my illness or swollen belly. She always closed her letters by mentioning that she couldn't wait to be reunited with Dad so that he could help her raise teenagers. She also expressed hope for finding polio treatments for me.

Dad was super organized and focused on having us join him in the United States. His first letter included detailed instructions about what he needed from us. He asked for copies of birth certificates, medical records, and additional photos. In his first letter, he asked how I was doing, particularly since he had heard about my malnutrition. My weight at the time was similar to a three-year-old child, not a ten-year-old.

When Mom and I went to the post office to mail the copies of our birth certificates, the postage cost was more than we had brought with us. We returned home and borrowed money from our neighbor to send the documents.

We received the first "care package" from Dad; it was like opening Christmas presents. He sent us Dove soap, toothpaste, toothbrushes, Alka-Seltzer, Bengay, and Pepto-Bismol. The Alka-Seltzer and Pepto-Bismol were sent to help my stomach pains. The Alka-Seltzer tasted horrible; I only tried it once. The Pepto-Bismol tasted good and worked like magic. The Bengay was for my leg pains.

The package also contained treats like chewing gum and chocolate M&M candies. Mom gave the Communists at the post office some of the gum so they would process the inspection of the package faster. We also shared the gum with neighborhood kids. The M&M chocolate candies had melted, but they were heavenly.

We sold items that we didn't use from Dad's care package in the marketplace. He included two large bottles of Tylenol. Medicine and medical care in Vietnam were a rarity and considered a luxury. We sold Tylenol tablets one at a time in the market. We also kept some Tylenol at our home for our personal use and for our neighbors. Our home felt like a medicine dispensary station at times.

Dad sent two packages each year, and we eagerly looked forward to receiving them. He knew that we did not have much clothing, so occasionally he sent fabric. My sister was an excellent seamstress and made each of us a shirt from the fabric. We always took a photo of our new shirts and mailed the photo to Dad.

Dad sent money as often as he could. This helped us buy some extra food and daily necessities. Money was not sent directly to us or through the banking system because we would never see the money. We utilized what was referred to as the black market to receive money from Dad.

There were several different techniques for getting money to our family. Sometimes, Dad gave money to a Vietnamese family in the United States, who would then contact their family in Vietnam to provide the money to us. These transactions occurred late at night or early in the morning under cover of darkness. We used coded language in our letters. The phrase "celebrate Chinh's birthday" meant money would be arriving for Dad's brother Dinh and Dad's father.

Dad had heard stories of Vietnamese in America hiding money in toothpaste containers, within the corrugated sides of cardboard boxes, and inside appliances and shipping the hidden money to their families in Vietnam. Sometimes, the hiding places were discovered by the Communist officials inspecting packages, and, sometimes, families accidentally threw away items that included hidden funds. My father helped take apart a transistor radio very carefully to hide $2,000 for boat passage funds. He placed a dummy capacitor on top of the actual capacitor and ensured that the radio still operated. The funds made it safely to Vietnam and enabled a friend's brother to escape by boat.

Dad sent the packages from a Vietnamese supermarket in San Antonio that provided shipping services. Once the care packages arrived at the Vietnam airport, they were opened and inspected. It was common for items to be taken. Dad included a list inside the package of everything he had packed, so we knew what had been taken.

In one of my letters to Dad, I told him how much better I felt after taking Pepto-Bismol. I called it the miracle medicine. After that, each package he sent contained several bottles of Pepto-Bismol. Imagine my surprise when one of the packages he sent was a wheelchair for me; this was a huge luxury, and I felt a strong surge of love and protection from across the tremendous distance that separated us.

In addition to being extremely careful about our written correspondence with Dad, we faced significant daily challenges. For Vietnam, the war between the North and South ended in 1975, but it was immediately replaced by war with our neighboring country, Cambodia.

Cambodian leadership changed two weeks before the fall of Saigon. The new Cambodian regime under Pol Pot named itself Democratic Kampuchea, and the Khmer Rouge began attacking Vietnam. The first attack occurred on May 1, 1975, on the Vietnamese island of Phu Quoc, barely twenty-four hours after the capture of Saigon.

The Khmer Rouge began massacring citizens in what are known in history as the killing fields. We heard horror stories from neighbors and friends about what was happening in the country next door to us. In hushed tones, we learned that all citizens in Cambodia were forced to become working peasants. Businessmen, educators, doctors, Buddhists, and foreigners were killed.

Vietnam invaded Cambodia and captured the capital city of Phnom Penh in 1979. During the Cambodian-Vietnamese War, my brother, Quang Phuong, moved into his teen years. This meant that he could be recruited at any time to join the Vietnam Communist Army. Vietnamese soldiers were needed to occupy Cambodia. We were continually worried about unannounced visits to our home, in which he could be yanked from the safety of our family and placed on the front lines.

Dad's father, Grandpa Ong Noi, had fought against the Communist Viet Minh during the First Indochina War, so we were wary of the Communist government and military force. Bribery was a common practice to keep young men from being recruited into the Communist military. Dad sent money to Mom to bribe *Cong An* from placing Quang Phuong into service. Thanks to the power of corruption, Mom was told ahead of time about an upcoming roundup of young men. Quang Phuong escaped to Uncle Truc's house in Bien Hoa Dong Nai. We breathed a sigh of relief because he had dodged the "draft."

One night, I awoke to the sound of neighborhood dogs barking crazily. I knew that something bad was happening. Quang Phuong quickly climbed out the window onto the roof. As I looked out another window, I saw armed men carrying flashlights and pounding on doors. This was a military-recruiting roundup. We felt betrayed because we had greased the skids to avoid this nightmare.

Sensing that he might be discovered on the roof, Quang Phuong quietly moved to the deep branches of our neighbor's mango tree, which brushed our rooftop. He stealthily hid himself from the waving flashlights. The armed guards pounded on our door and entered our home without being asked. They quickly walked through every room and looked under each piece of furniture and behind every door and curtain. They stepped outside into our yard and slowly used their searchlights to inspect every inch of our roof. When they didn't find Quang Phuong, they moved on to the next house.

Each day brought a different challenge. Vietnam occupied Cambodia for ten years, from 1979 until 1989. The threat of Quang Phuong being forcefully taken from our family and placed into the military was a steady drumbeat of danger. He constantly looked over his shoulder.

We had found out that Dad was alive in 1980. In his letters, he mentioned the Orderly Departure Program (ODP), created in 1979 by the United States to allow immigration of Vietnamese to

America. The intent of the program was admirable, but the process was incredibly long and complicated due to strained relations between Vietnam and America. Vietnamese often fled the country by boat in search of a better life because the immigration-approval waiting period was torturous.

The ODP office of the United States was established in Bangkok in January 1980. Once we knew that Dad was alive, we didn't realize that it would take almost ten years before we would be reunited; the total time of separation was close to fifteen years.

Once Dad located us, he completed the US forms to begin the process for us to immigrate to America. First, he had to become an American citizen, but the process mandated that he wait until a visa number was available before he could pursue becoming a US citizen. Once he received the visa number, he became a US citizen in January 1983. He was proud to call the United States his home.

In February 1983, Dad completed the Immigration and Naturalization form to confirm that he was a US citizen and to reinforce his request for his family to join him in America. Dad offered to also list his brother Dinh on the documents requesting immigration to the United States. Dinh had just gotten married and thought it was best if he remained in Vietnam, so he declined Dad's offer.

There were times when I became discouraged about how long reunification efforts were taking. It didn't seem like we were ever going to leave Vietnam. As an example, it took three years before Dad could begin the process of becoming a US citizen. Three stinking years. We had already spent five years believing that Dad was dead. Then we had to wait another three years for the immigration process to begin. At this point in time, it had been eight exhausting years, and we were at the beginning of the reunification process.

Daily life continued to be abysmal in the 1980s. During this decade, the Orderly Departure Program suffered from a series of stops and starts due to strained political relationships between the United States and Vietnam. The rate of approved departures slowed to an agonizing crawl. Due to economic sanctions, repressive regime programs, famine, poverty, and the war against Cambodia, hundreds of thousands of Vietnamese desperately wanted out of the country. They viewed fleeing Vietnam as their only hope.

The continued, exhausting delays depleted our energy and enthusiasm about leaving Vietnam through the ODP process. My brother decided to take things into his own hands and attempted to escape by boat. Dad sent money for the planned escape. In carefully coded language about money for Quang Phuong to attend welding school, Dad's letter to the family was clear that only Quang Phuong should attempt welding (escaping by boat) because there were horror stories about the dangers of welding (women being raped, killed, or captured by pirates while fleeing by boat).

Mom found a group of people who were organized and had the resources to help Quang Phuong escape. The entire process was very secretive. As a family, we had to be extremely careful about our actions and conversations. After six months of coordination, it was time for Quang Phuong to travel to a predetermined destination. It was a twelve-hour walk to the coastal city where he was housed in secrecy with ten other people. After arriving at the home, he tried to sleep for a few hours. Under the cover of darkness came the next portion of the journey.

The eleven travelers walked to the location of the canoe. They couldn't walk together, or they would raise suspicion, so they each had a planned route and a time to meet. The plan was to board the canoe that would take the group to another boat. The second boat would travel farther out to sea and transport the travelers to a larger fishing vessel.

The group slipped into the canoe with ease and pushed off from shore. Trouble came at the transfer to the second boat. Suddenly, a bright searchlight was aimed at the boat. The local secret police, *Cong An*, spoke into a bullhorn and instructed the escapees to put their hands in the air.

Quang Phuong and the rest of the group were placed in jail. As prisoners, their heads were shaved so that the public would know that they had attempted to escape. Mom had sewn money into the hem of Quang Phuong's pants; his captors quickly discovered the cash, as well as other hidden valuables sewn into the clothing of other travelers. Mom rode in a van, *xe lam*, for many hours to the coastal city of Rach Gia and paid bribery money to get Quang Phuong released from jail.

Because escaping by boat was a family affair, I knew that Mom talked with Quang Phuong about escaping again. One of the lessons he learned during his first attempted boat escape was the need to carry food with him. Luggage wasn't allowed on these risky departures, so he needed to carry some food in his pockets.

Mom made lemon sugar candy that could be placed in a baggy and stored easily in his pockets.

When Mom purchased a large bag of sugar and many lemons, I suspected something was up. She asked me to help make candy for his trip. Mom spread a thin layer of sugar on a tray and asked me to squeeze the juice of the lemons on top—taking care to remove the seeds. She placed the tray on a window ledge, where the sun helped the candy harden. Luckily, the window ledge was partially hidden by our neighbor's mango tree so that it wasn't easily viewed by neighbors.

My sister, Linh Phuong, also became despondent at the lengthy process for us to be with Dad in the United States. Despite Dad's warnings that she should not try to escape by boat, she felt strongly about taking the risk. Because Quang Phuong's attempt at escaping by boat had not been successful, the organizers, *vuot bien*, agreed to take both Linh Phuong and Quang Phuong for the price of one person.

Quang Phuong and Linh Phuong were met by the same misfortune as the first failed boat escape. It smelled like a setup. Luckily, Linh Phuong ran away and escaped her captors. It took her over fifteen hours to get home from the coastal city. She ran through ditches and farmland and then caught a ride in a van, *xe lam,* to get home. She burst through the front door with a wild look of terror on her face. She was covered in mud from head to toe.

Quang Phuong wasn't as lucky. He was placed in jail again, had his head shaved, and sat in lockup until Mom received funds from Dad. Mom made the long trek to release Quang Phuong with bribery money. Corruption and extortion had been commonplace in Vietnam for decades. There were many unscrupulous people who profited from families scraping together their life savings to try to escape.

We had several relatives who were successful in leaving Vietnam by boat. Aunt Kim's twin boys are three years younger than me. I lived with Aunt Kim, her twins, and Grandma Ba Ngoai when my mom, brother, and sister were forced to relocate to farm the Trang Bom countryside. Aunt Kim's husband came from a wealthy family and had relatives who fled Vietnam in 1975; their relatives lived in California.

At age twelve, the youngest twin, Binh, escaped Vietnam by boat with his dad. They spent three years in a refugee camp in Malaysia on Bidong Island before being approved to move to the United States. Their relatives in California sponsored their move to America.

The other twin, Vinh, escaped by boat and arrived at the same Malaysia refugee camp at age fifteen. He also spent several years at Bidong Island. Aunt Kim did not escape by boat; she was approved for departure in 1993 through the Orderly Departure Program and joined her husband and twin sons in California.

We did not have access to much news while living under Communist rule. We heard stories about successful escapes by boat, but we also heard many tragic tales about deaths and piracy at sea. It seemed that many Vietnamese felt it was better to die trying to escape than to not try at all. The taste of freedom was worth the risk.

Communist security forces lectured about the dangers of trying to escape by boat due to the possibilities of rape, beatings, piracy, and death. However, the hope of a new life seemed much better than remaining in Vietnam. Later, I learned that the United Nations High Commission for Refugees (UNHCR) estimated that between two hundred thousand and four hundred thousand Vietnamese died at sea.[9]

For those who survived the boat passage, oftentimes they were unwelcome on the shores of Southeast Asian countries. Some countries chose to push the boats loaded with refugees back into the ocean; others held the refugees as prisoners and then repatriated them back to their home country of Vietnam, Cambodia, or Laos.

This chapter of my life felt like an emotional roller coaster. The exhilaration of learning that Dad was alive and the incredible hope of being reunited fueled my energy, dreams, and imagination. I spent endless hours visualizing our family together again.

The low points caused great despair. Military-recruiting round-ups in the middle of the night, news of Khmer Rouge atrocities and genocides—particularly those targeted toward Vietnamese—tragic tales of boat escapes, the daily grind of poverty, and lack of nutrition tested my resolve to be strong.

Letters from Dad inspired me because he wrote about endless opportunities in the United States. He personally reinvented himself by attending college and working in a different industry. I became determined to excel at school so that I could attend college also.

I began dreaming and hoping about my future.

CHAPTER 10

Family Expansion

Our immigration request to be reunited in the United States with Dad had been in process since the early 1980s. As the decade was coming to a close, we weren't sure if we were any closer to actually seeing him.

In the first few years after Dad located our family, we were super excited about seeing Dad. I imagined what Dad looked like and what America was like. I wondered if the United States had any Vietnamese food. Dad sent letters describing his life in Texas, but there weren't enough details for me to imagine a complete picture.

One friend at school had a treasured, hidden comic book that she secretly shared with me. We knew that Communists did not support reading comic books, so we were careful when we looked at it. The cartoons in the comic book depicted cowboys riding horses and wearing cowboy boots and cowboy hats. The comic book scene was based in Texas, and I wondered if that was what life was like in the United States.

In the late 1980s, the Communists started allowing some movies from countries that were allies. We watched movies from the Soviet Union, East Germany, Hungary, and Poland. Occasionally, I saw some western movies that were approved by the Communists.

Each of Dad's letters reminded us to focus on learning English while we were waiting on approval for immigration to the United States. I began learning English in the sixth and seventh grades. Dad sent money for us to learn English from a private tutor who taught classes in the evening. Teachers who spoke English supplemented their meager teaching salaries by holding ESL classes.

During seventh grade, my teacher asked me if I wanted to represent our school in district competitions in English and literature. I readily agreed to participate. I did not receive any trophies or awards for competitive events while I was in seventh grade. During eighth grade, I also represented my school in district-wide competitions in English and literature. I ranked in the top ten.

When I participated in these competitions, I often heard people in the audience exclaiming, "That girl over there who is squatting is bright and competitive." Comments like this boosted my spirits because I wanted to prove that people with disabilities are capable and talented. I beamed when I saw that Mom was proud of me—especially when her friends praised me and said that their kids looked up to me as a role model for studying hard and excelling in school. I excelled at middle school, sixth through ninth grades. Every year, I received achievement awards called *hoc sinh tien tien.*

During my middle and high school years, I helped many of my classmates with studying and English homework. Even now, some of them still mention to me that they passed English due to my help. I loved learning and wanted to continue my education. I took the exam that would determine if I could progress to high school. I passed the test easily. The high school was closer to our home than the elementary and middle schools.

When I was in tenth grade, my head teacher, Mr. Bach, noticed how difficult it was for me to climb the high school stairs. He asked me detailed questions about the stairs and my typical day at school. He recommended to the principal that the school move some classrooms from the third floor to the first floor, where administrative offices were located, so that it would be easier for me to get to class. The principal agreed, and the classrooms were relocated. I am still in contact with Mr. Bach almost thirty years later. He was observant, asked questions, and took action. He stood up for me.

While I was in high school, Linh Phuong was attending college. She rode her bike each day to the university in Saigon. She was studying to be an elementary school teacher. There weren't many areas of study that were offered in college. Teaching and engineering were the primary majors that were offered. Linh Phuong paid for her college classes by working as a seamstress on nights and weekends.

By the time I was in twelfth grade, I was trying to determine what I wanted to do with my life. One of my wealthier friends with an interest in medicine showed me how she dissected a frog. The frog's heart was still beating during most of the dissection. It fascinated me tremendously, but I knew that we didn't have the money for me to seriously consider a career in medicine.

I had another motivation for wanting to pursue a medical career. I was sick most of the time when I was a child; when people looked at me, they told Mom that I wouldn't live past my sixteenth birthday. Whenever I heard that, I pictured myself becoming a pediatric doctor to heal and find cures for childhood illnesses.

It was challenging pursuing higher education and determining employment choices within the Communist regime. People who received good jobs and went to excellent colleges were typically associated with the Communist Party, or they had funds to bribe officials in the university system. Our citizenship documents in Vietnam classified our family members as *my nguy* and *nguy quan*, which meant that Dad had been in the South Vietnam military and that he had worked alongside Americans.

Every year, high school graduates who wanted to attend college had to pass an exam in Ho Chi Minh City. There were two parts to the exam. The first part of the exam was based on school subjects such as math, science, English, and history. Topics on social morality and political indoctrination were also included on the first part of the exam.

The second part of the exam was an assignment of points based on the student's family history for the past three generations. Family members who had been part of the South Vietnam military, worked with or for Americans, fought against the Viet Minh in the Franco–Viet Minh War, or participated in other revolutionary actions against communism ended up with fewer points assigned to their exam scores by the Student Recruitment Bureau.

Those with lower scores typically attended lesser-valued universities and ended up in lower-paying jobs, such as teaching. Linh Phuong was accepted into a college, where she was studying to become an elementary school teacher. Our family knew that her job prospects after college would be limited due to Dad's occupation.

I took the exam that indicated whether I could progress on to college. I was thrilled when I received the news that I had passed. I applied at the local college where most first-year students attended, and I was accepted.

While I focused on school, my brother grew weary of trying to escape Vietnam by boat. He determined that we were wasting Dad's money with unsuccessful attempts to leave the country. Quang Phuong channeled his frustration and energy into learning new skills. He began earnestly focusing on the printing business. He opened his own business and spent seven days a week, twelve hours a day, silk screening T-shirts and printing banners and signs.

Quang Phuong had two to three close friends. They had grown up together and were almost inseparable. One day, his friends introduced him to a beautiful, shy girl named Ngoc Dung. Ngoc Dung and her mom sold vegetables at the Xom Moi marketplace. Ngoc Dung came from a large family; she had five sisters and two brothers. She was known as being one of the quieter members of her family. Quang Phuong and Ngoc Dung both attended school until the ninth grade and then started working rather than continuing their education.

After dating for about a year, Quang Phuong decided that he wanted to marry Ngoc Dung. He wrote a letter to Dad and shared his plans with Mom. Dad was concerned about Quang Phuong's interest in getting married and objected to it because the immigration paperwork was already in process. To add another person's name to the immigration paperwork meant starting the process completely over. Dad emphatically told Quang Phuong not to get married because of the amount of time our family had already invested in the possibility of being reunited.

Quang Phuong pleaded his case with Mom, who was more understanding because she knew Ngoc Dung and she saw that the two of them were madly in love. Mom had me write a letter to Dad explaining that she had had a heart-to-heart conversation with Quang Phuong, but she couldn't stop him from getting married. The letter also indicated that Ngoc Dung would move in with our family after the wedding.

The Vietnamese engagement ceremony is called *Le An Hoi*, and it usually occurs six months before the wedding. It is the official announcement that a couple is in a serious relationship, and it's a time when both families come together to welcome the couple into each other's family. It also strengthens the relationship between the two families as they begin planning the wedding. Quang Phuong and Ngoc Dung had a small, private engagement ceremony with close friends and family.

Before the wedding, each family chooses representatives to lead the traditional ceremonies. In Vietnamese culture, the first grandson is a favored child. Mom contacted Dad's father, Grandpa Ong Noi, to see if he and Uncle Dinh could both be representatives for Quang Phuong during the wedding ceremony. They were thrilled that Quang Phuong was getting married and started planning their trip from Ban Me Thuot in the Central Highlands to Saigon. Mom also asked Uncle Truc, on her side of the family, to be one of Quang Phuong's representatives.

Decorations for Vietnamese weddings are amazing! Before the wedding ceremony, friends and family members create a beautiful framed entryway in front of the doors at the bride's family home and at the groom's family home. The entryway frame is made with coconut and palm leaves. At the top of the entryway into the home, a red-painted board with yellow letters is placed. The words on the board at the bride's family home say *Vu Quy*, which means "farewell." There is a farewell ceremony for the bride before the procession moves to the groom's family home. The board above the groom's family home says *Tan Hon*, which means "welcome." There is a welcome ceremony when the bride's procession arrives at the groom's family home.

On the Saturday before the wedding, the procession of the groom's family to the bride's family home occurs. The procession of the groom's family is in a specific order, with the first person being the representative of the groom, typically followed by the groom's father, the groom, and then the rest of his family and friends.

With a huge smile on his face, Grandpa Ong Noi proudly led the groom's procession to Ngoc Dung's family home. Behind him were my two uncles, our family, and Quang Phuong's close friends. As is our custom, we lit many incredible fireworks to announce our arrival at the bride's home. Her family responded with their own dazzling display of fireworks. The street in front of the house was ankle deep in firework remnants.

In Vietnamese tradition, the groom's family prepares gifts that are placed in big, decorated tin trays. The decorated trays are filled with gifts of fruit, nuts, and cash. The gifts of food and money represent unity and happiness. The gifts are covered by red cloth, which symbolizes luck and happiness for the couple. The gifts represent the formal request from the groom to receive the bride.

When the procession arrived at Ngoc Dung's home, Grandpa Ong Noi knocked on the door. The senior representative of the bride's family opened the door and exchanged traditional wedding greetings with Grandpa. Quang Phuong presented the caravan of gifts to the bride's family. Ngoc Dung's female friends and relatives lined up in front of the house to receive the gifts. Quang Phuong was then granted permission to receive the bride, and Ngoc Dung came out of her house dressed in a breathtaking *ao dai*.

Ngoc Dung wore a gorgeous, deep-red, majestic *ao dai* with an elegantly embroidered Chinese phoenix, *Phuong Hoang*. The phoenix symbolized grace and prosperity. Then, as all Vietnamese brides do, she added a sheer, white-lace, long cardigan called an *ao choang* over her *ao dai* on her wedding day. Her outfit was red for good luck, and it was trimmed in magnificent gold embroidery. Ngoc Dung wore a round-shaped headpiece called *khan dong* that matched her stunning *ao dai*.

Because our ancestors are worshiped, respected, and treated in holy ways, the next element of the ceremony began in front of the bride's ancestor altar. Quang Phuong and Ngoc Dung lit incense sticks, *nhang*, and asked permission from her ancestors to bless their union. Then Quang Phuong and Ngoc Dung bowed to her parents and thanked them for raising and protecting Ngoc Dung. Next Quang Phuong and Ngoc Truong solemnly bowed to each other.

Once the formalities of the ceremony were out of the way, the feasting and partying started. All of Ngoc Dung's neighbors had planned and cooked for several days to feed the large crowd. We ate and drank until late in the night.

The next day, Sunday, was the bride's procession to the groom's home. Members of the groom's family who did not take part in the previous day's events lit firecrackers to celebrate. Once the firecrackers stopped, my mom led Ngoc Dung into the house as a symbol of welcoming her into our family. Ngoc Dung was followed by her family members and friends. Quang Phuong and Ngoc Dung stood in front of our family's ancestral altar and repeated a similar ceremony from the prior day. Ngoc Dung was formally introduced to Grandpa Ong Noi, Uncle Dinh, Uncle Truc, and other family members during the altar ceremony.

Our neighbors and relatives helped us put together an incredible feast for Quang Phuong and Ngoc Dung for the ceremony at the groom's family home. We set up tables outside in our yard and several neighbors' yards. A typical wedding-party dinner is a twelve-course meal, so we had been preparing and planning for this event for quite some time. We roasted a pig that we chopped into small pieces and served with sticky rice, *xoi gac*. We also cooked Vietnamese sausage, *gio*, pork, and chicken. We served cold cuts, *nem* and *cha nuong*, and many different types of soups and stews. My favorite dishes at the ceremony were curried chicken and roasted quail. Then we had massive amounts of delicious desserts and plenty of alcohol. The party continued until the early morning hours.

In addition to the ceremonies at the bride's home and the groom's home, there was a Catholic church service where Quang Phuong and Ngoc Dung exchanged vows and wedding rings. Both were dressed in white for this sacred religious ceremony.

It felt exhilarating to celebrate a new beginning! I felt lighter than air watching Quang Phuong and Ngoc Dung exchange their wedding vows and look lovingly into each other's eyes. I longed for Dad to be able to be with us, but I knew that it wasn't possible.

Grandpa Ong Noi rode Quang Phuong's motorcycle during the two weeks that he stayed at our house. For an elderly man, he zipped around like he was drinking from the fountain of youth. Mom worried about Grandpa riding the motorcycle so fast, but Uncle Dinh told her that Grandpa would be just fine. It almost felt like we were a complete family again.

Shortly after the wedding, my brother's partners in the printing business exited the enterprise because they were accepted to immigrate to the United States. Quang Phuong invited Ngoc Dung's family to join him in the printing business. With the help of her brothers and sisters, it began growing quickly.

Later in the year, we received exciting news—Ngoc Dung was expecting a baby. Her due date was in December 1989.

Shortly after hearing the news about Ngoc Dung's pregnancy, we received a phone call from the ODP office that operated from the American Embassy in Bangkok, indicating our family was going to be interviewed by the ODP office in Ho Chi Minh City to determine if we could move to the United States.

Quang Phuong's reaction to the possibility of going to America was swift and forceful. He adamantly stated that he was not leaving Vietnam. He did not want to leave Ngoc Dung and his unborn child behind.

Mom and Dad insisted that Quang Phuong should come to the United States and then sponsor his wife and child to join him in America. My parents were concerned that removing Quang Phuong's name from the immigration petition document could cause agonizing delays for the rest of the family.

Mom spoke with Ngoc Dung's father and indicated that if Quang Phuong came to the United States, it would be relatively easy for him to petition for Ngoc Dung and his child to join him. Mom stated that if Quang Phuong remained behind in Vietnam, it could be difficult, and there might be additional delays with a request for the three of them to immigrate to America.

Mom implored Ngoc Dung's father to speak with both Quang Phuong and Ngoc Dung and to think about the potential future for his unborn grandchild. Ngoc Dung's father spoke with Quang Phuong and Ngoc Dung, and they begrudgingly agreed to continue the process, even though it meant that they faced potential separation.

I was nervous about our interview at the Orderly Departure Program office that would determine our fate. Would we be reunited with Dad, or would we be kept apart? What type of questions would be asked? What were the right answers, and what were the wrong answers? I peppered Mom with questions, but she didn't know what to expect or how to prepare.

When we arrived at the office building, it looked large and foreboding. As we entered the office, I was doing my typical squatting walk where I embraced one knee with the hook of my elbow, moved my foot forward about four inches, and then repeated it with the other knee. I hopped onto the chair across from the official's desk. He looked incredulously at me and in perfect Vietnamese said, "What's wrong with her?"

My jaw dropped to the floor. I had never heard or seen an American speak fluent Vietnamese. He seemed alien to me. Mom replied, "She has polio." Then he asked us why we wanted to move to the United States. Mom told him that we had been separated from Dad for over fourteen years.

I thought that I was dreaming when I heard the next words out of his mouth, in excellent Vietnamese: "Congratulations! You've been approved!"

CHAPTER 11

Goodbye Saigon

Fourteen years later, in 1989, a different suitcase sat on the floor in the corner of the living room. It was a large, shiny, aluminum suitcase with unique features—four rolling wheels and a pull handle. It was filled to the brim with hope of my new future.

Some days, I was super excited about moving to America. Other days, I was depressed and didn't want to think about saying goodbye to my friends, Grandma Ba Ngoai, Aunt Kim, Uncle Dinh, Grandpa Ong Noi, Uncle Truc and his family, and our neighbors. I didn't know what America would be like. I had only seen a few photos from Dad. I knew that the house we would be living in was made of brick because I had studied the photo he sent us. I looked at it inch by inch, trying to discern any small detail that I might have overlooked. I tried to imagine myself living in that house. Finally, we would be together as a family.

I thought back to 1975 and how I had been prepared for a new future when, instead, my world was turned upside down. I feared that the same thing would happen again. I had recurring nightmares where my suitcase was just out of my grasp and I tried desperately to reach it. If only I could walk and run, I could catch my suitcase and hold fast to my dreams.

Since we had heard the magical words, "You've been approved," things moved fairly quickly. We were allowed to bring one large suitcase with us. Mom bought each of us a large, silver, aluminum suitcase with wheels. We had never seen wheels on a suitcase before. Each suitcase had a lock so that our belongings would be secure. As a family, we could also pack a total of two medium-sized boxes for clothing. We were given permission to bring Dad's blue hard-case valise with us.

The suitcase was the size of a large steamer trunk; there was an engraved nameplate on top with Dad's name and address in San Antonio. Reading Dad's engraved name brought back a flood of memories of his blue hard-case valise. His valise represented joy and sorrow. Over the years, it had signified comfort when he arrived home from work. When Dad's valise was brought to our family and we were told that he had died, his suitcase symbolized tragedy. I kept his suitcase in my dresser drawer to store memories and keep hope alive. As we were packing to move to America, I was thankful that we had received permission to bring Dad's valise. I still have his suitcase today. It sits on top of my dresser as a reminder of the hopes and dreams that I have packed throughout my life.

While we were preparing to move, I kept asking myself and Mom a lot of questions. How could I possibly pack my entire life into one suitcase? How would I know what to bring and what to leave behind? What was truly important?

It was a strenuous process to reduce my belongings to fit into one suitcase. My biggest regret was not bringing the school yearbooks that I had created for fifth through eighth grades. They represented my creativity; they demonstrated the power of believing in someone. Mr. Nguyen, my fifth-grade teacher, had seen potential in me and unleashed it through his words of encouragement and support.

Our relatives and friends planned many goodbye celebrations where we laughed, cried, sang, and promised to stay in touch. Mom looked like a princess at each of these parties with her gorgeous *ao dai*. Behind her smile and positive attitude, she seemed hesitant about her new life. I saw her quietly sobbing at home. She was leaving everything and everyone she knew. Vietnam was her home.

Quang Phuong and Ngoc Dung tried to drink in every moment with each other. They were always together and never more than a few inches apart. Ngoc Dung cried a lot. We tried to comfort her by saying that she and the baby would be reunited with Quang Phuong. We also gently reminded her that continually crying was not good for her unborn child's health.

The baby was due four months after our departure date, and Quang Phuong would be thousands of miles away when the baby arrived. He had moments of repressed rage at the timing of our move.

The morning came when we left our home for good. Aunt Kim moved into our home as we were leaving. It felt good to know that our family history would continue in the home where we had worshiped and honored our ancestors.

The first portion of the trip was a bus ride to Tan Son Nhat Airport in Ho Chi Minh City at 6:00 a.m. Mom rented a bus so that our family and friends could ride with us to the airport. There were fifty people on the bus, and the mood was jovial. We were headed on a grand adventure, and our friends and family celebrated with us.

This was my first time on an airplane and my first time out of the country. As we flew to Thailand, I looked out of the plane window at the lush green fields and the waves crashing on shore. I put my finger to my lips and whispered, "Goodbye, Saigon."

Unfortunately, I ate too much food on the airplane, and I got motion sickness. I closed my eyes and tried to calm my stomach. When we landed at the airport in Thailand, we were transferred to a bus. The bus stopped in front of a large, four-story building that was being guarded by police. I was going to try to get off of the bus in my awkward squatting motion when a Thai lady spoke to me in fluent Vietnamese. "Please stay there. I'll get you a wheelchair."

The building was set up exclusively for ODP travelers. We spent a week there. It was like a refugee camp set up in a building. We were given several vaccinations and documents so that we could enter the United States. All ODP travelers had to wear ODP name tags and lanyards around their necks during their stays at the refugee camp and during all airline flights. I assumed it was a way to keep track of us. It made it easy for other people to recognize us at the airport so that they could guide us and help us get to the correct terminal.

Our next stop was in Paris, France. A tall pilot carried me on his back and gave me a signal to wrap my arms around his neck so that he could walk faster in order to quickly get us to another terminal in the Charles de Gaulle Airport. Then we boarded a huge airplane that took us to John F. Kennedy Airport in New York City.

We entered the customs area at Kennedy Airport, but we did not understand much English, despite the English tutoring we had received. Luckily, there were people helping all of us with ODP badges so that we could claim our luggage and understand the customs process. Then we had to give them back our luggage. It was confusing to us.

One airline employee helped us at the terminal counter and then pushed me in the wheelchair to our next gate. He asked me, "Where are you heading to?"

I didn't understand what he was asking, so he asked again and added hand gestures to demonstrate his question. I decided that it was a good time to test my English skills, so I replied by pronouncing, "Tex-at." He had no idea what I meant. He asked me to write it on a piece of paper. After I had written Texas, he burst out laughing and pronounced it for me. It was my first time using English in the United States, and the interaction with him is a sweet and funny memory.

Our next flight was to San Antonio, Texas. There weren't any people with ODP name badges going to San Antonio. It seemed like many ODP travelers were headed to cities in California. It felt like we were on our own. We didn't have anyone who could translate for us to help us understand what we needed to do.

By now, we had been traveling for over eighteen hours, and we were exhausted. My motion sickness had returned, so I didn't eat much. I sipped on a little bit of orange juice and water. I felt like I didn't have any energy left at all.

When the plane landed, we tried to exit, but the pilot stood in our way and was saying things to us we didn't understand. We were confused, angry, and bone tired. The pilot kept gesturing, but we still didn't know what he was saying. Then the pilot went to the cockpit and returned with a map that he carefully unfolded. He kept pointing to a spot on the map labeled New Orleans. Next he pointed to a place on the map called San Antonio. Through the map, hand gestures, and some partial English spoken by Quang Phuong, we arrived at the conclusion that we had landed somewhere else other than San Antonio. The pilot gestured to the seats on the plane and showed us that we should stay in our seats.

About an hour later, other passengers boarded the plane, and we left New Orleans, headed to our final destination of San Antonio. We landed in San Antonio about 11:00 p.m. There were few people in the airport. We looked bedraggled and haggard. Luckily, there was a wheelchair waiting for me on the Jetway.

In honor of Dad, Quang Phuong wore my father's military hat for our arrival in San Antonio. This hat had been part of my father's personal belongings that were delivered to us when we were told that Dad had died in a helicopter crash. Mom was wearing her best *ao dai*, while Linh Phuong and I were dressed in what we felt was appropriate Western-styled clothing. We were wearing the shirts Linh Phuong had sewn from the fabric Dad had sent us. We wanted to be fashionable, even if we were exhausted.

Then we saw Dad! It was a feeling I'd never had before. Time literally stopped. Mom, Quang Phuong, and Linh Phuong had walked out of the terminal ahead of me. I followed behind a few minutes later, being pushed in a wheelchair by an airline employee. My heart burst with joy when I saw Dad standing by the terminal door. Dad and I hugged for a long, long time. It was an emotional moment filled with ecstasy and joy. We basked in the glow of finally being together as a family. And then we all started talking at once to share stories of our lives. It was the ultimate sense of fulfillment.

Dad introduced us to several of his friends who were with him at the airport. Dad told us that he was going to cook steaks for us at home. We weren't sure what he meant by steaks, but I noticed that his friends said that they would join us at home for the meal.

The steaks tasted fantastic. Dad's friends thoroughly enjoyed every bite of their steaks and told us that our dad cooked the best steaks in town. I was so exhausted that I fell asleep on the couch while everyone talked. I partially woke up when Dad carried me to my room.

It seemed like the world had shifted on its axis when we arrived in America. Life would never be the same for us again. Around the globe, life was changing for millions of people.

Four months after we arrived in the United States, the Berlin Wall came down, and, within one year, West and East Germany were unified. During the next several years, Communist regimes in Hungary, Poland, Romania, and Czechoslovakia crumbled. Within two years, the Soviet Union dissolved into independent states. The Cold War had come to an end, and communism had started to shrink.

CHAPTER 12

A Stranger in a Strange Land

When we landed in San Antonio, it was late in the evening, so we didn't see much of the city. For the first few weeks, Dad drove us around. He showed us grocery stores, schools, public libraries, movie theaters, restaurants, hospitals, and the post office. Everything was so different and new to me: food, people, lifestyle, language, transportation, and street configurations. I felt like a stranger in a strange land. It seemed like I was starting my life all over again.

During these drives, I was amazed at how the highways were built and the layout of traffic flow. I had never seen access roads; it was a new concept to me. Dad stopped at rest areas that were clean with gorgeous landscaping. Dad took us to the River Walk, the San Antonio Zoo, SeaWorld, and the Japanese Gardens. My mouth was continually wide open with amazement as I tried to soak it all in.

I didn't see any cowboys or horses. Texas wasn't what I had imagined based on the comic books I had read in Vietnam. I was surprised to see so many cars; it seemed to be the only mode of transportation. Houses looked like mansions. I had never heard of fast food restaurants. Ordering food from a car and driving off while eating a meal seemed odd. I did not like the taste of the food at these unusual fast food places. All of my senses were on overload; it was overwhelming and exhausting.

Our home was filled with appliances that we didn't know how to operate. Dad showed us repeatedly how to use the dishwasher, washing machine, dryer, vacuum cleaner, and computer. Daily life felt strange; it was filled with constant learning and tension.

In addition to a new country, community, culture, and house, we were trying to adjust to being a family again. The last time we had seen Dad was in 1975; we were children, ages five, eight, and ten. We were now adults: ages nineteen, twenty-two, and twenty-four. Mom had spent the past fourteen years being our mother and our father and ensuring that there was food on the table. She was independent and proud that she had kept our family healthy, alive, and together. She raised three children who were well mannered and resourceful.

We didn't know Dad very well. It felt weird trying to build a relationship with my father when I remembered so little about him. Each of us struggled in our own way to create a bond with Dad.

We had hopes and dreams about being together as a family. Visions of togetherness had fueled our imaginations while we waited for our reunification petitions to be approved. The intersection between fantasy and reality collided quickly in our home.

The first explosion occurred between Dad and my brother. Quang Phuong was extremely homesick and missed his wife. He continually berated himself for leaving her behind while she was expecting their child. Quang Phuong was used to being the master of his domain and the head of his household rather than being thrust back into a parent-child relationship.

Dad wanted Quang Phuong to complete the ESL and GED classes and then go to college to become an airplane mechanic. Quang Phuong wasn't interested. Quang Phuong wanted to work and earn money in preparation for supporting his wife and future child when they arrived in America. Dad strongly believed that education was the pathway to a better life. Their differences of opinion were loud and challenging. We moved through our daily lives acting as if a truce had been constructed between Dad and Quang Phuong when, in fact, there wasn't one.

The explosive fireworks between Dad and my brother were a contrast to the slow burn of a dormant volcano between Mom and Dad. A volcanic eruption takes a long time to build up. Magma is the molten rock that pushes itself up the main vent of a volcano very slowly. Dormant volcanoes are ones that appear quiet or inactive, but they are capable of erupting.

The magma in my parents' relationship was the discussion about whether Mom would work. She was used to working and earning an income, and she wanted to continue to work and provide for the household. She was not interested in sitting idle in our house. Her passionate independence reminded me of the Helen Reddy lyrics, "I am woman; hear me roar."

Dad felt that Mom wasn't listening to him. He perceived her to be hardheaded while he was offering her a much-improved lifestyle. Mom wanted to work so that she could send money back to her brothers and sisters in Vietnam. Dad angrily stated that Mom should focus on helping her family here in the United States rather than sending money back to Vietnam. Dad wanted Mom to stay home, cook, and take care of the house while he worked and my brother, sister, and I attended school.

The cultural collision within our home created battle lines. Quang Phuong and Mom were entrenched on one side of the battlefield, and Dad was stationed on the other side. Linh Phuong and I were quiet bystanders who purposefully did not choose sides. The peace agreement in our home occurred when Dad agreed that Mom could work.

Dad reached out to his friend who owned a Vietnamese restaurant and asked if Mom could work for him. Mom worked in the kitchen of the restaurant cleaning and preparing vegetables. The restaurant owner felt that Mom worked too slowly, and her restaurant career came to an end.

There's an expression about winning the battle but losing the war. That's what happened with Mom and Dad. Mom's work experience ended, but that didn't solve the serious relationship issues that were building and straining like vapor pressure before a volcanic eruption.

Dad was burning the candle at both ends. In a house with five adults, he was the only one who spoke fluent English and had a driver's license and a car. He had recently received a promotion at work and was working long hours. A basic task like a trip to the grocery store required Dad to explain the layout of the aisles, the location of specific items, and how to pay with American currency. He was running himself ragged trying to take care of everyone's needs.

Dad had high expectations for each of us. He had worked extremely hard in Vietnam and in the United States. He'd earned minimum wage as a cook in South Dakota. When he worked at the television repair shop, he sent thousands of dollars to us in Vietnam for boat escapes, bribery money, and daily expenses. He'd felt disadvantaged when he arrived in America because his English wasn't good, but his work ethic and desire to continually learn helped him earn a living. He felt that he had to work much harder than those around him just to be considered equal.

For the past nine years, Dad had thought about how each of us could be successful in America. He wanted us to learn English, get a driver's license, obtain a college degree, and become financially independent. He also encouraged us to become US citizens. Quang Phuong was already focused on becoming a citizen to help expedite having his wife and unborn child join him.

When we arrived in America, I was surprised at how fluently Dad spoke English. He had learned English while in Vietnam and had been speaking primarily English since arriving in the United States. We teased him that his Vietnamese was a little rusty, when, truthfully, each of us had a long way to go to learn English. My brother and sister bragged that they knew enough English until they took an English proficiency test at the local community college and flunked.

Dad immediately enrolled Quang Phuong, Linh Phuong, and me in ESL and GED classes. GED certification was required before we could enroll in college since it was difficult to assess high school graduation proficiency between Vietnam and the United States.

Dad encouraged us to Americanize our names. He said that Americans had difficulty pronouncing our names correctly. The Vietnamese naming convention lists a person's last name first. Because Americans do the reverse and put their first names first and their last names last, Dad said that he was often being called by his last name. Dad Americanized his name and changed it from Tran Van Chinh to Chinh Van Tran.

After thinking about Americanizing their names, Quang Phuong chose the name Peter since Phuong and Peter both start with *P*. Linh Phuong changed her name to Lynn because Linh and Lynn are pronounced the same.

I tried several different attempts at a name change. I tried shortening my name to Thu and also to Hang; both were often mispronounced. One time at school, one of my classmates suggested an American name for me: Susan. I liked the sound of it and adopted it. One afternoon, I was driving an electric scooter that I had borrowed from the disability services center at school, heading toward the cafeteria. I heard someone shouting, but I continued to the café. One of my classmates rushed to my side and said, "Hey, I called your name, but you just ignored me."

I replied, "I didn't hear you call."

He said, "I called you Susan."

I didn't even think twice and answered, "No, it's Thu Hang."

And then I realized that the name Susan wouldn't work. I decided to simply put my two names together; I became Thuhang rather than Thu Hang.

Even though Dad was demanding about assimilating into American culture, he was also well connected with many Vietnamese people in San Antonio. He had founded and was president of the San Antonio Vietnamese Association. He worked extremely hard to keep Vietnamese culture intact within our community. He inspired me to believe that I could be proud of my Vietnamese heritage while learning about American culture and norms. He taught me to cherish both Eastern and Western cultures.

When Dad had heard that we were approved to move to America, he immediately researched polio treatments and surgeries. He spoke with several doctors ahead of time and set up appointments for me to meet with them once I arrived in San Antonio. Within my first thirty days of being on US soil, I was examined to determine whether I would ever stand up and walk.

The possibilities of my new life stretched beyond my wildest dreams and imagination.

CHAPTER 13

Standing Up and Looking Forward

The first doctor I visited in San Antonio was Dr. Rick Barohn, a neurologist at the University of Texas Health Science Center. Dr. Barohn completed his medical and neurology residency at Wilford Hall USAF Medical Center at Lackland Air Force Base in San Antonio.[10] Dad had met with Dr. Barohn before I arrived in America. The two of them hit it off instantly due to their Air Force connection. Dr. Barohn was warm, friendly, and gregarious. He confirmed my diagnosis as polio and referred me to Dr. Bob Jones, a physiatrist.

A physiatrist is a doctor who specializes in physical medicine and rehabilitation for patients who have movement or mobility impairment due to illness or injury. Physical medicine and rehabilitation physicians have extensive knowledge of nerves, muscles, bones, and the brain. When I visited Dr. Jones, he evaluated my range of motion while I demonstrated how I moved around. His notes from our visit indicated that my left knee was severely deformed and bent at a thirty-five-degree angle. An interpreter in the examination room ensured that we understood each other accurately.

Dr. Jones said, "I wish I had seen you when you were ten or eleven years old. We could have improved your mobility and maybe helped you walk normally."

With a quiver in my voice, I tentatively asked him, "Can you help me walk now?"

He replied, "I think we can definitely help you walk; it will probably be with the aid of braces and crutches."

With tears welling up in my eyes, I softly said, "Thank you. This has been my dream for a long time."

Dr. Jones stated that an orthopedic surgeon would have to straighten my left leg. This required surgical intervention consisting of cutting the bone above and below my knee and inserting steel bolts and screws so that my knee could bend and move correctly so that I could be in an upright position. He mentioned that I would spend six months in a leg cast and possibly up to one year in physical therapy.

Because he specialized in rehabilitation of the whole individual, he advised that standing upright after squatting on the floor for the past seventeen years would change my breathing and communication, which would impact my speech capabilities. He indicated that I also needed speech therapy.

Dr. Jones asked if additional physicians, residents, and medical students in graduate school could meet me. He said that they rarely had patients with polio. Soon the examination room was filled with doctors asking many questions and watching as I demonstrated my movements to get across the floor. Throughout my surgery and recovery, I received many visits from different doctors and residents.

Dr. Jones recommended Dr. David Anderson, an orthopedic surgeon. Dr. Anderson concurred with Dr. Jones's assessment and scheduled my surgery at the Medical Center in San Antonio. I couldn't believe that I had only been in the United States for two months, and I was scheduled to have surgery to help me stand upright and walk. It was a dream come true!

The night before my surgery, we had a special dinner at home as a celebration. Dad cooked his specialty—steak and baked potatoes with all of the toppings. Mom was extremely nervous about my surgery and was constantly praying the rosary and asking God to bless me. Peter and Lynn were excited for me. We all sat down to a great meal and thanked God for our blessings.

As I packed my suitcase for the hospital, I thought about the symbolism of new beginnings, adventure, expanded horizons, and, most of all, hope. I packed lightly because I was going to be in the ICU for two to three weeks, and then I would be moved to a rehabilitation facility for several months.

As I was wheeled into the operating room, I noticed that the room was filled with many physicians and nurses. Dr. Anderson also pointed out the medical school residents standing above us on the second floor watching through a plate-glass window. I felt a little bit like a celebrity. The operation took a grueling ten and a half hours. My family waited nervously in the waiting room to hear from Dr. Anderson.

When the doctor approached my family, Dad jumped up from his chair and asked how I was doing. Dr. Anderson indicated that the surgery was a success, but I would be heavily medicated for the next few days to ensure a smooth recovery. I barely remembered the male nurse who checked on me in the recovery room.

I tried to stay focused and open my eyes, but I quickly fell back to sleep.

The first thing I remembered after surgery was hearing Dad's voice. I felt like his voice had interrupted my dreams. The nurse told Dad to try to wake me up by gently shaking my body while shouting my name. I slowly opened my eyes and saw Dad in front of me and the nurse off to the side. They both exchanged some conversation I couldn't understand. I knew that I was cold and shivering.

"Dad, I'm too cold," I spoke softly like I had lost all of my energy.

Dad said to the nurse, "She's cold."

The nurse grabbed two blankets and put them on me to keep me warm. I continued staying in the recovery room for another ten minutes. The nurse pushed the hospital bed out of the recovery room while I was shaking and my fingers were blue. Dad told the nurse that he was concerned about me because I was still bluish in color. The nurse reassured him that I would be fine once I got to my hospital room.

When I got to my hospital room, I started feeling a little bit more like myself. I was hungry but couldn't eat anything. The nurse gave me some crackers and sipping ice only. She helped me sit up and raised the bed. At that moment, I saw a humongous cast on my left leg. I looked like the abominable snowman on one side of my body.

When the nurse left, Dad asked me if I needed anything. I said, "I just want to sleep." We talked briefly about my surgery. My dad couldn't stay late that night because he had to sleep and go to work in the morning.

Dad stopped by the hospital every day on his way home from work. My mom, brother, and sister came to visit me a few days after the surgery. Since the medication made me sleepy all of the time, I hardly remembered who came. Sometimes, Dad's friends came to visit; I exchanged a few words and apologized if I suddenly dozed off. Most of the time, his friends visited when Dad was there after work, so Dad talked to his friends and coworkers while I slept. I received so many flowers, balloons, and gifts that brightened up my hospital room.

As I was recovering from surgery, the pain was excruciating. It felt like a sharp object near my knee. One afternoon a few days after the surgery, the male nurse came in and explained the medicine I could request if my knee had too much pain. I said with a determined voice, "I'm all right now." He smiled slightly as he backed away and left the room. Then, sure enough, I had terrible pain around 10:00 p.m. while trying to sleep. I signaled the nurse with the call button by my bedside rail. The male nurse came in and saw my tears streaking down my face.

He quietly asked me, "Would you like some pain medication or a shot?"

"A shot, please," I replied without any hesitation.

After two weeks in the hospital, Dad knew that I was craving Vietnamese food badly, so he brought in some food Mom had cooked. It was one of the best dinners I've ever had. The nurses smiled broadly as they saw me eating with gusto.

The day I was transferred to Warm Springs Rehabilitation Hospital, Dad was at work, so no one in my family was with me during the ambulance ride. I was worried about what was happening to me. I wondered where they were taking me. What were they going to do with me? The male nurse saw that my face looked concerned; he told me that I was being transferred to another hospital. I understood what he was saying but couldn't respond back or carry on a conversation due to my limited English. I just nodded my head. He wheeled the gurney to the back of the ambulance.

It was a short drive. When I arrived at the rehab facility, it reminded me of a luxury hotel. It was gorgeous. The building architecture was elegant, with arches in different colors of brick. There were beautifully manicured grounds outside, so some of my walking activities included fresh air. When I was pushed to the entrance of the rehab facility, I saw the hospital that I had arrived from in the distance.

Dr. Jones and Bev Hermann oversaw my recovery journey. Marianne Smith was my physical therapist. They put me through grueling exercises that had me in tears. The first time, Marianne put a big belt around my waist and helped me stand up. I lost my balance, but she helped me maintain a standing position with my crutches. My left leg was still in a hard cast. My right leg had a removable brace.

The moment I stood up, it felt like my brain was swirling around in my head. I saw the room and all of the objects around me at a level I had never seen before. It was a strange, thrilling, and emotional moment. I was in awe at the kaleidoscope of colors and sights in front of me.

Dr. Jones oversaw my rehabilitation efforts, including physical and speech therapy. I didn't realize it at the time, but the brain is critical for good balance. My head felt funny; sometimes, it felt heavy, and, other times, it seemed fuzzy and lightheaded. I never knew that balance was determined by both physical skills and thinking abilities.

Marianne was very kind and patient. She showed me how to move with my crutches by extending one leg at a time. When I lifted my leg to make a move, I felt like a baby learning how to take a wobbly first step. It was surreal and exciting at the same time. I lost my balance and fell down. Luckily, I landed on my rear end on the exercise mat nearby. Marianne was concerned that I had gotten hurt. I didn't get hurt, but my knee was in such pain that I couldn't continue with physical therapy that day. I learned that progress would come one slow step at a time.

One weekend, while I was walking on my own along the bar rail, Dad walked in with Mom; they sat down to watch me walk. I saw sheer happiness on their faces. Mom started crying. I knew that she was crying tears of happiness because I wouldn't have to squat on the floor anymore. Dad was thrilled and proud because I would have a bright future and live independently. When my brother and sister came to the rehab hospital and saw me walking, they were beaming.

I continued to work hard because I wanted to be able to walk and be independent. During my speech-therapy sessions, I began learning English. After three months in the rehabilitation facility, it was time to go home. I continued physical therapy for another year.

I was surprised when a reporter with the *San Antonio Express-News* asked if he could write a story about me. With the help of our priest as an interpreter, the news reporter visited Warm Springs Rehabilitation Hospital and took a picture of me and Marianne. He also interviewed all of my doctors.

The newspaper article ran on Friday, December 22, 1989. One of my doctors was quoted as saying, "She had an unfortunate childhood, but she has some luck going for her now. She's a feisty little lady."[11] The doctor also said that in later years I might suffer from post-polio syndrome, which causes the body to wear out faster, and that I might require a wheelchair.

The article ended by mentioning that it would be the first Christmas in fourteen years that our family would be together for the holidays. As Dad drove me home from the rehab hospital, the song "I'll Be Home for Christmas" was playing on the radio.

Standing up and looking forward felt like a Christmas miracle.

CHAPTER 14

Family Evolution

Our first Christmas together was magical. Mom and Dad decorated our house with sparkling Christmas lights, an evergreen Christmas tree, and a small wooden nativity scene. It looked like a winter wonderland.

We attended Christmas Eve Mass and felt so grateful for our many blessings. Our prayers had been answered, and we were together again as a family. I was standing upright and walking with the help of crutches and braces on both legs. And we had a new member of the family, Tran Quang Huy. Peter and Ngoc Dung's son was born in Vietnam a few days before Christmas in 1989.

In 1990, Peter, Lynn, and I all passed our GED exams. We began attending San Antonio Community College and continued to take ESL classes along with other courses. Our school schedules were not similar because I had extensive physical-therapy appointments and Peter and Lynn were both working.

While Peter was attending college, he got a job at a grocery store, which helped him learn the American way of business. Peter didn't feel like he could handle a job and college classes, so he dropped out of college. When he decided to stop going to college, one of Dad's friends helped Peter get a different job at a friend's framing business. Peter quickly learned the framing business and how to manage the shop. He wanted to be prepared for the arrival of Ngoc Dung and his son, Quang Huy.

In the meantime, Lynn had been attending San Antonio Community College for ESL classes but also decided to drop out. Lynn had always been an excellent seamstress. Dad contacted another friend of his who owned an alterations store, and Lynn started working there. She met a handsome young man named Son Hoang Nguyen, and they began dating. It developed into a serious relationship; soon they were talking about the possibility of marriage.

Mom struggled the most with our move to the United States. She had a hard time adjusting to a new life and new culture. She wasn't able to grasp English, and she didn't learn to drive. She missed her brothers and sisters in Vietnam terribly.

Watching the metamorphosis of my parents over the years was akin to watching a caterpillar become a butterfly. Mom was a submissive housewife in the early years of her marriage. Due to the war and our hellish circumstances, she became fiercely independent and determined to eke out a living for our family. She had used her skills to sell and make items in Vietnam, and she was the head of our household at that time. She focused on the present, the here and now.

Dad, on the other hand, constantly focused on the future. He thrived on learning new things, solving complex issues, accepting daunting challenges, and constantly improving himself. He also expected the same of those around him. It felt like my parents had outgrown each other, and the chasm felt wider and deeper each day.

I asked Peter and Lynn their thoughts about our parents' marriage. Peter's perspective was that it was Mom and Dad's issue, not ours. He didn't want to get involved or be a part of any discussion. Lynn was always the peacemaker in our family, and she felt that they just needed more time together.

I'm the one who is direct and up front. I kept debating about whether to talk with Mom or Dad about their marriage. At the tender age of twenty, I wasn't exactly an expert on the topic of marriage, but I knew that I was watching a marriage disintegrate right before my eyes.

I tossed and turned at night as I thought about potential approaches to the conversation. I felt like it would be better for all of us if we could honestly discuss what was going on with our family. I didn't have any solutions figured out; I just wanted to start the dialogue.

Then, one day, the opportunity presented itself; I seized the bull by the horns. Dad and I were the only ones in the house. I poured a cup of tea for both of us and invited him to sit with me at the kitchen table.

I sat quietly for several minutes with my hands interlocked underneath my chin and just stared at him. He kept looking back at me. It almost felt like a stare down. Finally, I said, "Dad, what's going on with you and Mom?"

He looked intently back at me. "What do you mean?"

"The two of you don't seem very happy."

He sighed heavily. "Things are strained between us. We don't see things the same way."

I told him that we all felt the tension. Then I told him that Peter, Lynn, and I would understand and support both of them if they needed to separate. I wasn't sure Peter and Lynn felt this way, but I believed that there was safety in numbers.

I don't remember the rest of the conversation. I mostly remember feeling a huge sense of relief talking about their troubled marriage. Little did I know that timing would play an important factor in resolving the conflict.

Peter was interested in moving out of the family home and finding his own apartment in preparation for his family moving from Vietnam. In Vietnamese culture, parents often live with their oldest son. It is the oldest son's responsibility to take care of his parents as they age.

My parents decided to separate, and Mom and Peter moved out of the house. My parents were civil and cordial to each other during this family transition and at all family events that have since transpired.

At the time of my parents' separation, I was trying to determine what I wanted to do with my life. My secret passion was to become a doctor. I had been so impressed with the physicians who helped me walk that I literally wanted to follow in their footsteps. I also remembered hearing our neighbors in Vietnam when I was first diagnosed with polio tell Mom that I wouldn't live to be sixteen. At that moment in time, I wanted to be a pediatric doctor to help children.

I spoke with a doctor at the rehab facility about becoming a doctor. I noticed that the doctors I saw did not have mobility issues.

I had to use crutches or a scooter to get around. It seemed like doctors were always pressed for time and constantly on the move. I also realized that my English would have to improve significantly if I wanted to be a doctor.

So, I started exploring other career paths. I knew that I needed a career that fit with my mobility needs. When I spoke to Dad, he encouraged me to study electrical engineering like he had. I took one course in electrical engineering and found it incredibly dry and boring.

I spoke with a career counselor at San Antonio Community College about my interest in graphic design; I admired all of the games, cartoons, and movies that were designed on computers. The counselor told me that the computer graphic design major was only offered at the University of Texas at Austin. At the time, we couldn't afford the cost of tuition and a dormitory room in Austin. So, I asked what majors were available at the community college that related to computers. She reviewed the list of majors and recommended computer science or management information systems. I chose computer science.

The career counselor at the community college also provided me with information about transportation services, called VIAtrans Paratransit Service, for people with disabilities. The counselor gave me the application form and helped me apply for passes on VIAtrans.

The VIAtrans bus had strict rules; it parked by the curb in front of each person's house and waited ten minutes. If the passenger didn't arrive in ten minutes, the bus left. The bus driver arrived at my house at 6:30 a.m. on weekdays; I was the first stop. I stayed on the bus for three hours as other disabled people were picked up from their locations. Some were dropped off at an activity center for people with disabilities. Due to my transportation needs, I signed up for classes that started after 10:00 a.m.

Each time a disabled person in a wheelchair boarded the bus, the loud clanking and slamming of the wheelchair lift being lowered and raised gave me a headache. The long drive and the tremendous noises caused a lot of headaches. I learned to adjust to it, but the headaches never went away.

Despite the challenges of headaches and loud noises, San Antonio Community College had incredible services for disabled people; it was the best I had ever seen. The college provided a center, staff, and counselors to help people with disabilities get to classes. Wheelchairs and scooters were available for disabled people to borrow. I frequently used a scooter to get around campus. The school never ran out of resources for their differently abled students. There was easy access to all of the buildings and classrooms.

One day, I chose a scooter to get to the computer lab. As I was driving it down the handicap ramp, the brakes weren't working; it felt like I was accelerating quickly and driving on three wheels. I screamed at people in front of me so that I wouldn't run into them; they moved to the side quickly. One of my classmates saw what was happening, and he quickly ran toward me and pushed a button on the scooter to disable it. It was a scary and fun moment. I swapped it out for a different scooter.

I took the VIAtrans bus for the two years I was at the community college. I made a few friends, and several of us transferred to the University of Texas at San Antonio, UTSA. There were four of us who carpooled to UTSA; we became close friends. UTSA also offered the same high level of services for disabled students as the community college, which helped me access classrooms easily.

During my last year at UTSA, I got my driver's license. I was so excited to have my license: it represented freedom and independence to me. When I got home, I told Dad that I had gotten my license, and now I could drive myself anywhere I wanted to go.

Dad responded that even though I had gotten my driver's license, I had not passed his driving school. Dad's driving lessons reminded me of military boot camp. I'd witnessed Lynn crying when Dad taught her to drive, and I was concerned that I would have the same experience. I did cry most of the time while he was teaching me to drive. In hindsight, I appreciate what he taught me because I have never had a driving ticket or an accident. He was the toughest drill sergeant—I mean, teacher—that I've ever had.

Once I had my driver's license and a car outfitted with hand controls, my daily schedule started with leaving home at 6:00 a.m. and returning home at 10:30 p.m. The commute to UTSA was far from our home, so I stayed on campus to attend classes, study, and work in order to maximize my time. Every night, I fell asleep and recharged, only to get up and do it all over again the next day. Dad kept reminding me that the time spent completing my education would be demanding, but it would be worth it in the long run.

While attending college, I became a US citizen and received a letter from President Bill Clinton:

I want to congratulate you on reaching the impressive milestone of becoming a citizen of our great nation. As you enjoy the benefits of American citizenship and assume the responsibilities that accompany it, you follow the many brave men and women who have sacrificed to establish and preserve our democracy over the last two centuries.

You now share in a great experiment: a nation dedicated to the ideal that all of us are created equal, a nation with profound respect for individual rights. The United States is a land of unparalleled natural beauty, vast opportunity, and freedom. It is home to people who have been drawn to our shores from all over the world and who share a common love for life and liberty.

Please join me in devoting your hopes, your prayers, your energies, and your labor to our common good and to the future of this wonderful country. Together we must strive to safeguard the freedoms we hold so dear, not only for ourselves but for future generations.

Hillary and I welcome you as a new citizen and extend our best wishes for much happiness in the future.

Sincerely,
Bill Clinton

During the same year that I became a citizen and received my driver's license, Peter received the news that Ngoc Dung and Quang Huy would be reunited with him in the United States. We greeted them at the airport with balloons and banners when they arrived. Quang Huy was an active toddler at two and a half years old, and he quickly adapted to his extended family in the United States.

Ngoc Dung missed her parents and her large family in Vietnam. It was a huge cultural adjustment living in San Antonio. It took her several years to work up the courage to learn to drive. She began calling her son an American name, Tony.

Lynn and Son announced that they were getting married. As a family, we planned their engagement and wedding ceremonies. The celebrations were in traditional Vietnamese style, and Lynn was a stunning, beautiful bride.

Our family continued expanding with the births of several nephews and a niece. My sister and her husband welcomed Sonny into their lives in March 1994. In 1996, we were blessed with two new babies in the family. Richie arrived first in May to proud parents Peter and Ngoc Dung. A few months later, my sister gave birth to Theresa in August. At this point in time, my parents had a total of four grandchildren: three boys and one girl.

While I was at the University of Texas at San Antonio, I revitalized the Vietnamese Student Association. I organized the leadership structure and created programs and policies. We grew to a group of over one hundred students. One of our most memorable events was a picnic at Canyon Lake, Texas, where we spent hours talking, eating, and enjoying each other's company.

In May 1997, I received my bachelor's degree in computer science from the University of Texas at San Antonio. It was a glorious, sunny day; my family cheered me on as I received my diploma. I was the first person in my family to receive a four-year college degree. Dad beamed proudly throughout the entire ceremony.

I was ready for the next step in my life.

CHAPTER 15

Celebrations and Sorrow

Life had settled into a rhythm. Peter and Lynn were busy working and raising their families. It had been eight years since we arrived in America; we had transitioned and assimilated into our new country and community.

Prior to graduating from college, I started searching for a job in San Antonio. I helped my sister with marketing plans for the alterations business she opened in 1996. I created 20 percent–off coupons to attract new customers. I helped in Lynn's business on the weekends, including assisting with the design and creation of a custom wedding dress. The customer loved her dress and told us that several of her wedding guests kept asking who designed it.

During my last year of college, I worked thirty hours per week for a professor at the University of Texas at San Antonio. The professor conducted research for a Houston hospital. I wrote code to read the scanned films of human brain cells so that the research information was easily accessible. I also supplemented my income by tutoring college students in algebra and calculus.

It wasn't long before I received a job offer from Sprint to be a software engineer at their Dallas office. It was an exciting opportunity to analyze and identify technical and business solutions, as well as to provide coding for the Sprint long-distance voice service and the digital subscriber line.

While I was in college, Mom moved out of my brother Peter's home and into the home of my sister to help raise Lynn's children while Lynn built her seamstress and alterations business. Dad and I had been living together in San Antonio for about four years. When I got the job offer from Sprint, I talked with Dad about whether he wanted to stay in San Antonio or move to Dallas. Dad had opened a frame shop while we were in San Antonio, but he decided to sell his business and move to Dallas with me.

Dad and I silently packed our suitcases and boxes as we prepared for our move to Dallas. We knew that we wouldn't be able to see our family as often as we had in the past. We had mixed emotions of sadness and excitement for the next chapter in our lives.

Although Dad and I lived five hours away, we traveled frequently to San Antonio for me to see Mom, for both of us to attend my nieces' and nephews' birthdays, and to spend time together at Thanksgiving, Christmas, and Tet. With our regular trips, the grandkids bonded and became close to my dad, their grandpa.

Dallas was our home for twelve years. I worked at Sprint for seven years and IBM for five years. At both companies, I solved complex business and technical issues. I utilized my skills in analysis, design, coding, and testing to develop integrated platforms. In addition to working at a corporate job, I became an entrepreneur and created websites for small businesses.

I wanted to be a catalyst for connecting the Vietnamese community in Dallas. Dad had been instrumental in creating a cohesive Vietnamese community in San Antonio, and I felt compelled to do the same. I am passionate about helping orphaned children in Vietnam, particularly those who are disabled. After researching the internet about organizations that help Vietnamese orphaned children, I found an organization in Dallas called Hoa Lu.

I learned that the Dallas Hoa Lu chapter was in the early stages of development; there were only four or five members. Once I joined, we quickly recruited additional members. I realized that we didn't have an official charter as a nonprofit organization, so I helped create one. In 2005, we hosted a fundraising event with a dinner that included a Vietnamese singer as entertainment. My team and I contacted many local businesses about sponsoring the event and purchasing tables and tickets. We raised thousands of dollars, which were sent to Vietnamese churches that take care of orphaned children.

I also decided to create an online Vietnamese community so that we could connect, communicate, and support each other worldwide. I partnered with two friends in California and built an online forum in 2005 called bensongmay.com.

Our site was a collection of Vietnamese stories, poems, photography, and art. But more importantly, it was an assortment of fabulous people. We built relationships that have endured for over a decade. We also organized multiple fundraising events in Southern California to help low-income children in first through fifth grades living in Vietnam who needed assistance with school tuition. After five years, I turned over the responsibility of the site because I had received a job offer from Walmart. I was moving to Bentonville, Arkansas, to work for the largest Fortune 500 company.

I had never visited or lived in Arkansas; Dad had lived for a few months outside of Ft. Smith, Arkansas, when he first entered the United States. He was excited that we were moving to the Ozark mountain region. I had read about the amazing growth of businesses, particularly in the vendor community, in Northwest Arkansas. More importantly, I was thrilled at the prospect of working on technological projects with tremendous scale and impact.

I almost had to pinch myself when I thought about growing up in war-torn Vietnam and now heading to work for the world's largest retailer. My primary responsibility was identifying risks and recommending design and test procedures for new projects while leading a team of twenty quality engineer vendors, both onshore and offshore.

What I remembered most about February 2011, in addition to being on an incredibly steep learning curve for my new role, was the freak snowstorm that buried Bentonville, Arkansas, in twenty-two inches of snow. Dad and our neighbors were continually shoveling snow from rooftops, iced-over trees, driveways, front porches, and sidewalks. I helped the snow crew by providing hot meals inside our warm, toasty house. The public schools had fourteen snow days during the winter of 2011.

During this freak snowstorm, the large tree that we had in front of our house split in half. The huge tree branches landed just inches from my dad's bedroom; luckily, he wasn't harmed. Our front yard and driveway were completely covered with downed branches. Fortunately, a landscaper was already in the area helping our neighbors with their fallen tree. The landscaper offered his services, but Dad insisted that he could chop the branches into firewood himself. It took my dad and the neighbors about three weeks to chop all of the branches. One of the reasons that we had purchased this specific home in Arkansas was because the beautiful tree in the front yard reminded us of the big oak tree in the front yard of our home in Dallas. Dad and I love the serenity of massive trees. Sadly, we learned that the tree in front of our Dallas home was taken down by the new owners.

Maneuvering in the snow is extremely dangerous for me. When I walk, I put all of my weight onto my crutches on each arm. If either or both of my crutches were to slip on ice or slide in snow, I would fall down immediately, and it would be next to impossible to get back up without some assistance. Luckily, technology has helped me be readily accessible without physically being in a specific location.

During the same year Dad and I moved to Arkansas, my brother and his wife welcomed a baby girl, Jackie, into their family. Jackie is much younger than her brothers, Tony and Richie. She is full of energy and feels like she can do anything that her brothers do. Dad and I spoil her with love and gifts when we visit because she is the youngest member of our family. I have always enjoyed being the baby of my family, so Jackie and I have a special bond because both of us are the youngest in our families.

Unfortunately, Peter's wife, Ngoc Dung, was diagnosed with diabetes shortly after Jackie's birth. Ngoc Dung had a heart transplant several years ago, but her health has continued to seriously deteriorate. She has lost most of her vision and is bedridden.

In the midst of Ngoc Dung's health challenges, life delivered a severe blow.

On Friday, April 24, 2015, my nineteen-year-old nephew, Richie Tran, was killed in a horrific car crash. It was one day before his high school prom and about a month before his high school graduation. He had already been accepted into the US Army and was excited about starting his military career and serving his country as his grandfather Chinh and his great-grandfather had done.

The grisly crash occurred around 9:20 a.m. when Richie tried to pass another car. When he accelerated, he lost control and drifted into heavy traffic in the oncoming lanes. His silver Honda convertible was T-boned by a black Chrysler. Richie was pronounced dead at the scene. The driver and two passengers of the other car were taken to the hospital with serious injuries.

My father received a call that morning from my brother. Peter was inconsolable, and it was hard to understand what he was saying. During the twelve-hour drive to San Antonio, I constantly thought about Richie and all of the wonderful memories. When we arrived at Peter's home, he collapsed in Dad's arms and sobbed uncontrollably.

Richie had a close group of friends. To honor Richie, his brother, Tony, and friends created and played a Rest-in-Peace video at his funeral service. The tribute video highlighting Richie's life was set to the song "See You Again," which was written by American rapper Wiz Khalifa and sung by Charlie Puth. The song was created as part of the soundtrack for the movie *Furious 7* as a tribute to the late Paul Walker, who died in a single-vehicle car crash on November 30, 2013. The song was released March 10, 2015, about a month before Richie died.

The poignant video included photos of Richie with his family and friends. Most of the photos showed Richie with his friends at church retreats. The photos resembled church youth groups like Dad used to lead. Richie as the Hulk at Halloween, sitting on Santa's lap, goofing off in a Hollister store, and wearing a Pikachu hat and backpack highlighted a young man with a zest for life. He demonstrated his athleticism, bulging biceps, and six-pack abs with several bodybuilding poses. The closing photo showed Richie standing next to his beloved silver Honda convertible. Audible sobs escaped the congregation as the video came to an end.

There was such an outpouring of love, prayer, sympathy, and support that I felt compelled to post a Facebook message to the thousands of people who had reached out to our family. I posted this message in loving memory of Richie:

Dear Friends,

On Wednesday, we said farewell to our beloved son, brother, grandson, nephew, and cousin to take the next journey of his life: traveling with God. With the outpouring of love, stories, and memories from Richie's friends, we were overwhelmed with pride about Richie. We were also pleased that his actions have touched and left positive impact on others.

Richie had always wanted to become a policeman since he was a child.

Whenever he was asked why, he always replied, "To protect the community." Later, in his young adult life, he wanted to join the military and be a marine. Because of his passion and curiosity about cars, he became a knowledgeable, skilled mechanic at the local car dealer while still attending high school full time.

God has plans for all of us, and Richie's destiny has come; therefore, it's time for him to go, to start his new journey. Richie will be forever missed; we will keep him near and dear to our hearts.

On behalf of my brother's family and our extended family, we sincerely thank you for calling, caring, and providing comfort, support, and prayers to our family during this difficult time. There are simply no words to fully express our heartfelt thanks for the sympathy you have extended toward our family. We are deeply grateful to you.

My niece, Theresa, and Richie were born the same year, and both were scheduled to graduate from high school at the same time. After Richie's funeral services, Dad and I stayed in San Antonio for a few days and then returned home to Arkansas. In June 2015, we drove back to San Antonio for Theresa's high school graduation. The principal called Richie's name posthumously at his school's graduation ceremony.

Life is filled with endless twists and turns. Sometimes, life's greatest celebrations, such as high school graduations and proms, occur at the same time as significant personal tragedies.

PART IV

CHINH

CHAPTER 16

Overcoming Obstacles

As Thuhang's father, there were times when I felt that I would never see my family again. After five years of searching, when I found out that my family was alive, it felt like I had climbed Mt. Everest. Mt. Everest is the world's tallest mountain at twenty-nine thousand feet above sea level. It rises into the stratosphere between Nepal and China. Everest is the ultimate destination for any mountaineer and is frequently used to evoke imagery about achieving goals that seem impossible.

During the prior five years, I had shared with friends, coworkers, and acquaintances my undeterred focus on locating my family. Some scoffed at the idea and told me to create a new life for myself in America. Others admired my goal but expressed realistic concerns about contacting family members within a Communist regime. And then there are Sherpas in each of our lives—those who believe in you and have the skills, imagination, and fortitude to propel you forward. Minh was my Sherpa. He never gave up on the possibility of finding my family. Minh became my adopted brother. I am forever grateful for Minh and his family and their unselfish desire to help me.

Learning that my family was alive galvanized me into immediate action. I am an organizer and a detailed planner, and I love to research solutions, so I immediately began investigating what needed to be done to bring my family to the United States. To obtain approval for a petition of application to sponsor my family for reunification, there were several requirements. First, I had to become an American citizen. Then I had to be able to prove financially that I could provide housing, food, clothing, school, health care, and employment for the first three years for all family members who were on my petition application. The information had to be verified that none of my immigrating family members would need public assistance from the United States.

I got to work right away on becoming a US citizen. The first step was to see if I was eligible to become a naturalized citizen. There were many questions to answer to determine eligibility status. My English-speaking skills were stronger than my English-reading skills, so I asked friends to help me read and understand the information. After submitting the naturalization application, the next steps included a background check and an interview. I became a naturalized citizen in January 1983.

I submitted the paperwork for reunification of my family and the confirmation that I had become a United States citizen. Then I waited and I waited and I waited some more. I had heard that the reunification process would take a long time, but I wasn't sure how long. I thought that the Orderly Departure Program that was implemented in 1979 would expedite seeing my family, but that wasn't the case.

In the meantime, I focused intently on performing well at work and improving my education. While working at the television repair shop, I attended San Antonio Community College and received my associate's degree in electronic theory. I was hired at Datapoint Corporation in December 1980 as a technician. Datapoint was originally known as the Computer Terminal Corporation (CTC). It was founded in 1968 in San Antonio; the first products were computer terminals that replaced teletype machines.[12]

The founders of Datapoint had worked together at General Dynamics as part of a computing contract team for NASA to help with President Kennedy's vision of putting a man on the moon.[13] Datapoint engineers created the architecture of the modern micro-processor chip that is used in personal computers.[14] Datapoint also created and patented one of the earliest videoconferencing systems, called MINX (Multimedia Information Network eXchange), which was used by the Pentagon.[15] I was fortunate to be one of the key engineers on the MINX project.

After a year and a half with Datapoint, I was promoted to lead technician and was responsible for troubleshooting and repairing more complicated boards on various disk drives. During this same timeframe, the internal newsletter at Datapoint featured an article about me and my work; it also mentioned that I was trying to bring my family to the United States.

In addition to working, I created the San Antonio Vietnamese Association and was president of the organization for nine years. I had several purposes in creating the Vietnamese Association: to develop a social network and activities for Vietnamese who had relocated to San Antonio, to remind younger generations of our heritage and traditions, and to help raise funds for boat people. For three consecutive years, we hosted a Tet Festival, where we cooked and sold over ten thousand spring rolls and shish kebabs. The local newspaper covered our events with photos and articles. Our membership grew to over one thousand Vietnamese. We raised more than $10,000, which we provided to a boat-refugee organization called Duong Song in Santa Ana, California.

In addition to working hard at my job, I continued my education. I had received my associate's degree and wanted to obtain my bachelor's degree. I applied and was accepted at Texas A&M and completed a course in basic electronics. But I found it too challenging to continue my education and work at a demanding career as well as actively lead the San Antonio Vietnamese Association. I decided to stop pursuing my education.

I was also active in my church; most of the congregation members were Vietnamese. We shared our meeting space with an existing church, but we continually ran into conflicts when the English service ran long. Our priest decided to utilize his garage for the Vietnamese Mass services. We quickly outgrew the garage and were looking at other options. Our priest called and asked me and several parishioners to look at an abandoned church on an acre of land. When we visited the property, I visualized a grand church. The others weren't so sure and recommended that the property not be purchased. I shared my vision with the priest and suggested that he buy the property. I told him that there was plenty of free manpower with the parishioners. At the next Mass, the priest announced that the property had been purchased, and I was overseeing the renovations.

I put together a group of twenty men and women to create a project plan to restore the church. A friend and I constructed an elaborate altar, while others used their talents in various ways. It took about five months to fully renovate the church. The archbishop and monsignor attended the grand-opening celebration. The archbishop cut the ribbon and provided the blessing. Then we delved into mounds of great Texas barbeque chicken, brisket, and pulled pork with all of the fixings—potato salad, coleslaw, and baked beans.

For five or six years, I led the youth group at our church. I felt a personal responsibility and commitment to the one hundred youth who attended our weekly sessions. I divided them into four groups and provided activities to each group. In addition to Christian teachings, I taught them about life—trust, integrity, love, respect, work ethic, education, and achieving your full potential. Part of my interest in being with young people was due to missing the time with Quang Phuong, Linh Phuong, and Thu Hang as they grew up.

When I saw people in need, I tried to help. One hot summer day, I noticed a young couple walking in the street in San Antonio. They had two small children with them. I pulled over and asked if they were from Vietnam. The man and woman replied yes and started crying. I invited them to get in my car. I drove them to my apartment and fixed them lunch. They ate like they hadn't had food in a while.

I told them that I would help them find a place to live. I contacted a friend of mine, and he took me to an apartment where twenty Vietnamese were already living. Then I asked my landlady if she knew of a one- or two-bedroom apartment. I mentioned that my friends and I would help with the deposit and initial rent.

After we located an apartment and several of my friends agreed to help financially, I told the man that I would help him get a driver's license and a job. I provided him with a loan for $1,200 so that he could purchase a car. He repaid me on time.

One night, I got a call in the middle of the night; the husband told me that he was headed to the hospital because his wife was in labor with their third child. I rushed to the hospital to be there with them. The doctor asked him to join his wife in the delivery room; this wasn't a typical practice in Vietnam. He turned to me and asked me to be in the delivery room with his wife. At first, I objected, but he insisted that I go with her. She gave birth to their third daughter while holding my hand in the delivery room.

I became close to his family and their three daughters. One time, his wife confided in me about her husband's drinking problems, which on occasion turned to abuse. I had a heart-to-heart conversation with him and poured all the liquor down his sink. I'm proud to say that his three girls are now grown women with careers and children of their own.

When I joined Datapoint in 1980, I didn't realize that I had joined at the height of the company's prosperity, and a downhill slide was on the horizon. As demand for our products increased, lag times slipped, and customers became unhappy. In early 1982, Datapoint lost $800 million in market capitalization.[16] In March 1985, corporate raider Asher Edelman took over Datapoint.[17]

Shortly thereafter, Datapoint spun off the service division into Intelogic Trace.

Luckily, I survived these massive changes and transitioned to Intelogic Trace. In June 1988, I was promoted to associate engineer. Typically, this role required a four-year college degree. My supervisor went to bat for me and outlined my eight years of work experience with the company, my associate's degree, and my four years spent on engineering functions, as well as being incredibly complimentary about my skills and abilities. I was thankful that my work ethic and expertise were being recognized and rewarded.

While I was eagerly waiting for my family to come to America, I became deeply concerned about the plight of boat people—those trying to flee Communist regimes in Vietnam, Laos, and Cambodia. It seemed like every day there were television images and newspaper articles about thousands of people dying at sea while seeking a better life.

In 1988, I became more distraught about the issues boat people faced because Thailand, Malaysia, and Hong Kong implemented stringent restrictions that treated refugees as prisoners. I almost quit my job so that I could move to the Asia region and help refugees. I spoke with a friend at the Indochina Refugee Action Center (IRAC) about my plans to assist refugees. He advised me to remain in the United States so that my application for reunification with my family wouldn't be impacted.

Prior to the policy changes in Thailand and Hong Kong, there was a White House vigil on March 27, 1988. Key leaders in refugee advocacy attended and spoke: Dith Pran, a Cambodian killing fields survivor; New York Congressman Stephen J. Solarz; and David A. Harris from the American Jewish Committee. Attendees of the vigil learned that over one million Vietnamese had fled their country since April 1975, and six hundred thousand had fled to America.[18]

Congressman Solarz told the crowd, "The six hundred thousand Vietnamese who have come to the US have enormously enriched the cultural, social, and economic life of our nation."[19] He continued, "If the United States is a beacon of hope and freedom to the people of Vietnam, the people of Vietnam are helping to contribute to the greatness of America."[20]

In closing, Solarz spoke from his heart: "Fifty years ago my people, the Jewish people, sought to flee from Nazi-occupied Europe. In their moment of greatest peril, we turned our backs on them. We sent the boats that carried them away, and six million died in the gas chambers and crematoriums of Nazi-occupied Europe. Have we not learned the lesson that all men are brothers and that we have a responsibility to all those who seek to flee oppression? Once again, people are looking for us to help. And once again, our government speaks with a very quiet and feeble voice."[21]

I was hopeful that refugee advocates would make inroads with the boat-people crisis. Southeast Asian countries were not the only countries struggling with the arrival of refugees; the United States experienced resistance to Vietnamese refugees. The American public was strongly opposed to letting Vietnam refugees into the country; polls showed support for welcoming Vietnam refugees into the United States at only 37 percent.[22] Racial tensions erupt-ed in Houston, Galveston, and Seabrook, Texas, as Vietnamese shrimpers clashed with white fishermen; a Ku Klux Klan group threatened the Vietnamese fishermen by sailing the seas in white robes and burning effigies.[23]

I have always been driven to help others and to continually have hope. Part of the reason I created the San Antonio Vietnamese Association and became involved with the Vietnamese youth at my church was because I wanted to create a sense of community where we could talk about the challenging issues we were facing. I wanted to demonstrate a path forward and help people assimilate into America and be successful. The immigrant experience can be so daunting; having others you can turn to makes the journey less difficult.

During the decade of the '80s, while I was waiting to be reunited with my family, it seemed like I was constantly on the go—whether it was complex projects at work, planning activities for the youth group, raising funds for boat people, attending college, or helping those in my community. Because communications were so slow and tedious between the United States and Vietnam, I didn't hear regularly from my family. When I did hear from them, their daily challenges were significantly more detrimental than anything I was facing.

I sent bribery money for my son, Quang Phuong, to keep him from being recruited into the military. Although I had proudly served my country, the conflict between Cambodia and Vietnam concerned me greatly. I didn't want to lose my son before I had the chance to reunite with him. I wanted him to have a better future. I did not want him serving in the Communist military.

Although I was proud and excited that my dad and brother represented Quang Phuong at his wedding, how I wished I could have been there with Quang Phuong.

Then I received a phone call that my family was going to be interviewed as the final step in the approval process for reunification. The news was electrifying!

CHAPTER 17

Becoming a Family Again

I wish I could tell you that our family's journey had a fairy-tale ending, but life isn't like that. Life is messy. Life is complicated. Life is filled with high peaks and low valleys. Some of life's adventures are soft, rolling hills with lush, green valleys, and other parts of life are sheer cliffs with deep chasms.

Once I knew that my family was coming to America, I immediately researched the possibility of polio surgery for Thuhang. I'd changed my health care coverage from single to family coverage in 1980 when I knew that my family was alive. Although I paid a higher health insurance premium for almost a decade, I wanted my family insured so that Thuhang could immediately be evaluated by doctors to see if she could possibly walk. I set up Thuhang's first doctor appointment within thirty days of her expected arrival date in America.

The most vivid memories of my life are seeing my family when they arrived in San Antonio. The first person I saw was Quang Phuong; he had grown into a young man and was wearing my South Vietnam Air Force cap. He was so handsome, taller than me, and had an engaging smile that lit up the airport. I gave him a huge bear hug, and we both started crying.

Then I saw Linh Phuong; she was a beautiful young woman with a touch of shyness. She was a spitting image of my wife, Lieu. Linh Phuong was as tall as Lieu, and they both had the same mannerisms, facial features, and gentleness. It was exhilarating to hold Linh Phuong in my arms.

Thuhang arrived next in a wheelchair. The last time I had seen Thuhang, she was five years old; now she was nineteen. She was full of zest and talked excitedly about the journey to San Antonio. Her eyes held a sparkle that spoke volumes about her resilient spirit. I couldn't lift her up and hold her in my arms like I used to when she was a child, but we hugged for what seemed like an eternity.

At last, Lieu and I embraced, kissed, and wept. I was overjoyed and completely overcome with emotion. Lieu was wearing a beautiful traditional Vietnamese *ao dai* with a colorful floral print. I felt such a tremendous relief to finally hold her in my arms. I had dreamt of this moment for a decade and a half, and now we were finally together as a family.

The challenges of being reunited with my family soon surfaced. We were more like strangers than family, yet we tried desperately to make it work. It eventually sorted itself out, but not without some heartaches along the way. The most defining moment during that time was Thuhang's surgery.

I remember it clearly, like it happened yesterday. As I prepared to take Thuhang to her first doctor evaluation in San Antonio, I thought back to 1975 and her new rattan suitcase with red trim sitting in the corner of our living room in Saigon. At age five, she had been set to travel to West Germany for a life-changing polio treatment when her dreams were disrupted. She had endured crawling and squatting along the floor for seventeen years, yet she had an incredibly cheerful disposition, and she managed her challenges like a true champion. The "baggage" Thuhang carries with her is light so that she can quickly adjust to new circumstances. She doesn't spend any time thinking about what could have, should have, or would have been—she focuses intently on the future and making the most of her life.

I fervently hoped that this time, when Thuhang packed her suitcase for polio surgery, her life would be significantly changed, and her dreams of being able to walk would come true. Despite all of the tragedies and challenging obstacles our family has faced, we have many blessings to celebrate. Seeing Thuhang walk was a miracle we had been dreaming about for decades.

Life is a series of transitions. As my children became adults, my role as their father shifted. I became more of a confidant than an authoritative figure with heavy influence.

My role changed substantially once Thuhang received her college degree. I have followed her career and moved to the cities where her employers are based. After living in San Antonio for over twenty years, I organized and planned our move to Dallas.

Later, as we prepared for our move from Dallas to Arkansas, Thuhang and I talked about my next chapter in life. I was in my late sixties; I wanted to stop working and focus on learning new skills. We decided that I would stay at home and pursue my interests in Eastern medicine, particularly acupressure. Acupressure is an ancient Asian healing art that was developed over five thousand years ago. Fingers are used to gradually press the key healing points, which releases tension, increases circulation, reduces pain, and stimulates the body's natural self-curing abilities.

My entire life, I have enjoyed helping others, whether neighbors, coworkers, homeless people on the street, or youth at church. Acupressure is another way I can help others by relieving their aches and pains. I have been able to help many friends and acquaintances with acupressure.

Even though I have lived in America since 1975, I still think about Vietnam. It has been over forty years since the fall of Saigon. I visited Vietnam in 2003 and met with several of my relatives, including my brother. It was great to reconnect after so many years. Although Vietnam has started thriving compared to several decades ago, there is still abject poverty. It was discouraging and disheartening to see firsthand how difficult daily life is in Vietnam. I am so grateful for my instinctual, last-minute decision to flee Vietnam in search of a better life.

I have witnessed the premature death of my mother, the atrocities of war, the debilitating polio diagnosis of my daughter, and the painful, lengthy separation of my family. Each turn of events forced me to determine how I was going to react and endure. I always focus on the future and acknowledge the things I am grateful for in my life.

Tragedy visited our family in April 2015 when my grandson Richie was killed in a gruesome car accident. I will never forget hearing Peter's voice on the phone as he tried to talk. It was a choking, rasping, horrid sound. I knew that something devastating had occurred, but I couldn't understand a single word he was saying.

I have seen many deaths, particularly while serving in the South Vietnam Air Force. I have witnessed the callous brutality humans can inflict on each other. But it didn't prepare me for losing my grandson at age nineteen. His future was just beginning.

As Thuhang and I drove from Arkansas to San Antonio, I kept thinking about my son, Peter, and the life he has lived. Peter grew up while I was often away fighting in the war; then I fled Vietnam, and he didn't have any direct physical contact with me for fifteen years. He had to leave an expectant wife behind when he came to the United States. His first son, Tony, was born without Peter living in the same country. Peter is an entrepreneur and owns his own business, which requires long hours. Peter's wife, Ngoc Dung, is critically ill, and now his middle child has died. He has endured tremendous hardship.

When I entered Peter's home that sorrowful day, he fell into my arms and sobbed uncontrollably. His body was shuddering so hard that I felt the need to hold on to him tightly and never let go. I knew that I couldn't lessen his pain, but I wanted him to know that I was there for him. And I always will be.

Life isn't always fair. We don't have control over some events that impact our lives. But we do control how we deal with the situations we encounter. I have never given up hope. The flame of hope is eternally ignited within me. I never gave up hope that I would be with my family again.

Determination drove me to create a new life in the United States. I knew that this great country was rich in opportunities. I didn't want to squander my chances. I believe that hard work and continually learning new skills can change lives. I cherish the spirit of independence in America. Our country is known for pulling yourself up by your bootstraps, and I believe that people can rise above the challenges that confront them.

However, sometimes, we need to give people the boots so they can pull themselves up by their bootstraps. I think about the young Vietnamese couple walking down the hot streets of San Antonio. I picked them up and gave them lunch in my apartment and found ways to help them—to give them basic boots so they could begin building their lives and pulling themselves up by their bootstraps. Without boots, there aren't bootstraps.

I am so grateful for the love of my family and for the wonderful blessings we have experienced. I also appreciate the people who provided me with "boots" when I needed help.

THUHANG'S AFTERWORD

I have had an interesting journey for the first four decades of my life, and I'm looking forward to what the future will bring. I am proud to be Vietnamese American with a blend of two different cultures. I am so grateful for Mom and Dad and their continued love and support.

Although I have faced extremely difficult situations, I have always looked for positive aspects of my environment. My dogged determination and perseverance helped me through obstacles and often provided insight into my inner passions and strengths. I had no choice but to continually reinvent myself, whether it was due to polio, war, Communist rule, or moving to another country. I kept reminding myself to put one foot in front of the other and continue moving.

The most important ingredient in life is hope. Without hope, the will to survive withers. I have always imagined a better future for myself. I knew that a better future was dependent on me and on actions I took and will continue to take. One of my favorite expressions is "if it is to be, it is up to me." I own my future, and I create the vivid picture in my mind of where I want to go.

One of the most powerful lessons I have learned was to not let others define me or place limits on what I could accomplish. Don't let others build a wall around you. Sometimes, we live up to or down to others' expectations of ourselves. Your personal goals for yourself should be higher than any other person's goals for you. When people felt I couldn't do something, I set out to prove them wrong.

When my parents chose my name, they thoughtfully and deliberately wanted my life to be full and bright like the autumn moon. I hope that I have lived up to their dreams. Their persistence and sacrifice in continually researching and trying different polio treatments literally and physically brought me to my feet.

My future plans are to create a nonprofit organization focused on providing resources for disabled children in Vietnam. I often think of teachers, like Mr. Nguyen, who believed in me and encouraged me to reach my full potential. I want to be able to inspire and help others who are differently abled.

Over the years, suitcases have held my dreams. My new rattan suitcase with red leather trim was packed to the brim with hope that I could walk again. Dad's dark-blue hard-case valise carried happy and sad memories with the role it played in my life. His valise was a secret source of comfort to me because of the photographs hidden inside. The one humongous, silver, aluminum suitcase carried my entire life's dreams when I moved to America.

When I packed my suitcase to go to the hospital for knee surgery, it literally held my heart inside. When Dad and I packed our bags to move to Dallas and then to Arkansas, we were excited and filled with hope for our new adventures.

As I am finalizing this book, Dad and I are in the midst of another move, another adventure. We are moving to Austin, Texas, where I will be working with the State Department of Texas. Dad says that we are riding our "metal horses," a term that he uses for cars, toward our new horizon. I feel that God is smiling down on me as I start a new job in a city that is much closer to my family in San Antonio. It is a dream job because I will learn ways to serve the people and the community of Austin. I hope to learn new skills that will translate into a future role where I can help orphans and the disabled in Vietnam.

I am so grateful to Dad for his unconditional love. His energetic enthusiasm as he plans and organizes each of our moves is inspiring to me. His sense of exploration and his willingness to be alongside me during each of our quests is amazing. He continues to protect and care for me.

Shed the baggage you don't need. Pack lightly, and enjoy your grand adventure.

READING GROUP GUIDE

1. What did you learn about the Vietnam War and/or South Vietnam that you didn't know?

2. How did the book change your perception of the Vietnam War and/or South Vietnam?

3. What part of Thuhang's personal journey resonated with you, and why?

4. What surprised you the most when you were reading the book?

5. If you had to choose the most important lesson Thuhang is trying to teach us with this story, what would it be?

6. Describe your reaction to Chinh's decision to escape South Vietnam. What decision would you have made, and why?

7. Describe your experiences with people who are differently abled and how this book will shape future interactions.

8. How does the immigrant experience of the Tran family compare with current events regarding immigrants and refugees?

9. If you could write one more chapter after the ending, what would you write?

10. How is this book connected to other books?

THANKS

We would both like to thank and give tremendous appreciation to the incredible team at Brown Books Publishing Group. Thank you to Milli Brown for believing the story needed to be told and encouraging us during each step in the process. A huge shout-out to our editor extraordinaire, Judy Hebb, for her insightful, spot-on, constructive critique; you made the book what it is today. Cathy Williams, LaNell Armour, Dru Bickham, and Abby Gregory Armstrong were fabulous in marketing the book to a wide range of venues. Katlin Stewart kept the trains running on time by overseeing the entire project. Kelly Werner and Leah Edwards played pivotal roles with video productions and press kit materials. Tom Reale, thank you for your sage advice and wisdom at many critical steps.

Thuhang: First, I would like to thank my mother and father from the bottom of my heart for their unconditional love and their continual sacrifices and for believing in me. My father, who always pushed me to continually strive for excellence, has made me the person I am today. My brother, Peter, and sister, Lynn, have been my steady rocks throughout my life; we have shed many tears of sorrow and happiness together. My extended family, including nieces, nephews, brother-in-law, sister-in-law, aunts, uncles, and cousins, has seen me through moments of joy and challenging obstacles. I honor my ancestors who came before me. I hope that families who are separated due to war, immigration policies, financial necessity, and other reasons can be reunited.

I am especially thankful to Mr. Dinh Van Suoc and his family for the extraordinary efforts they took to help with our family's reunification. Without their involvement, my life would have turned out very differently.

I'm grateful to all of the doctors, physical therapists, nurses, and speech therapists from San Antonio and Warm Springs Rehabilitation Hospital who were part of my journey. They shared with me the indescribable joy when I stood up and took my first steps after many years of crawling at ground level.

A special thank-you goes to the people who worked at the disability service centers at San Antonio Community College and the University of Texas at San Antonio. They were gracefully patient and helped provide me with assistance throughout my college years. I am grateful to have the support of friends Thong, Quang, and Dan, who invited me to carpool with them to UTSA for two years; the laughs we shared shortened the ride and created a lifetime of fond memories. A wholehearted thank-you to Dr. Kay Robbins, who believed in me and created opportunities for me with her projects so that I could gain experience prior to graduation.

I would especially like to thank my mentors, Sabrina Freeman, Craig McSherry, and Ronald Pinault. They noticed my talents and abilities and helped me grow professionally and personally. My sincere appreciation and gratitude goes out to each of them. They have taught me a lot.

To my colleagues and close friends from the companies where I have worked, thank you for your kindness and support throughout the years.

A special thank-you to Hua Wang for introducing me to Sharon once he heard my story.

That's where this book starts. Most importantly, I would like to thank Sharon for gracefully listening to my story and making it seem like time stood still during our initial conversation.

Sharon's unique personality established trust between us the first time we met. Thank you, Sharon, for helping my dreams come true with this book. I will forever treasure our friendship and partnership.

Sharon: This book would not have been possible without the courage, trust, transparency, and generous, warm spirit of Thuhang and Chinh. I am honored and humbled to have been invited into their lives. The retelling of their stories and the need to probe for details created the recurrence of nightmares for them. I am forever indebted to them for their kindness and their commitment to telling their story so that others can learn about life during and after war and as immigrants and refugees.

This book would not have happened without the serendipitous conversations and encouragement from Hua Wang and Kelvin Goss—a huge thank-you to both of you! Friends in the author community have been incredibly helpful with suggestions and advice: Allie Bowling, Tom DeWolf, Rich Harwood, Claudia Kennedy,

Peggy Klaus, Helene Lerner, Allyson Lewis, Nell Merlino, Sharon Morgan, Clifton Taulbert, and Rob Tenery.

Feedback is a gift, especially when it's thoughtful, specific, honest, and transparent. A special thank-you to Kevin Turner for always taking the time to provide direct, detailed feedback. Bob Ford has been a fabulous mentor due to his experience in Vietnam and as an author; his frequent phone calls encouraged and inspired me throughout this process.

Dr. Mohammad Bhuiyan and Bernie Milano are two trusted friends who have continually challenged me to dream big and take bold steps. Both are actively involved in making a difference in the lives of others by providing pathways through education and unique experiences.

Jose Villarreal is a tireless advocate and vocal champion for immigrants and immigration reform. His focus on developing understanding and cooperation across nations benefits all of humanity. Thank you, Jose, for being a beacon of light for others to follow.

Glenn Llopis celebrates the role immigrants play by driving an innovation mentality. Immigrants see opportunity in everything, anticipate the unexpected, and live with an entrepreneurial spirit. America benefits greatly from immigrant entrepreneurialism. Glenn, your time, energy, and passion fuels my spirit.

Thank you to my former neighbor, Rollin Ford, for setting the gold standard of care and compassion for everyone in the workforce. A special thank-you to Dr. Rohini Anand, a kindred spirit and thought partner regarding inclusion for all.

A tremendous thank-you to Bill Gates and the Bill & Melinda Gates Foundation for committing to polio eradication as one of their top priorities. Their technical and financial support of the Global Polio Eradication Initiative (GPEI) has accelerated targeted vaccination campaigns and routine immunizations. The end result has been a 99 percent decrease in polio cases.

Donna Nessmith and Kaye Cullum both provided peaceful, secluded environments where I could hunker down unseen and focus on writing—thank you! I have an amazing group of friends and colleagues who continually asked about the book and provided advice and support. I couldn't have completed it without you.

Thank you to my parents and siblings for providing encouragement and insights that helped shape the book; in particular, my sister Cindy Nooney, a fabulous author, was a key sounding board and a personal cheerleader extraordinaire. My children, Orin and Shannon, have participated in many conversations about the book, and I am always grateful for their perspective and patience.

Finally, the person I want to thank most is my husband, Craig. He is my lifetime soul mate; he has always been supportive of our adventurous life together, including the large amounts of necessary solitude required to write a book. Despite all my broken promises to play golf with him, he cheers me on towards the goal line.

NOTES

1. Associated Press, "Minh Surrenders, Vietcong in Saigon," *New York Times*, April 30, 1975, http://events.nytimes.com/learning/general/specials/saigon/surrender.html.
2. Le Ly Hayslip, *When Heaven and Earth Changed Places* (New York: Penguin Group, 1989), x.
3. Mark Lawrence, *The Vietnam War: A Concise International History* (New York: Oxford University Press, 2008), 55.
4. Ibid., 52.
5. Ron Steinman, *The Soldiers' Story: Vietnam in Their Own Words* (New York: Fall River Press, 1999), 267.
6. "Graham Martin," *Wikipedia*, https://en.wikipedia.org/wiki/Graham_Martin.
7. Sandra Bartlett and Joseph Shapiro, "At War's End, U.S. Ship Rescued South Vietnamese Navy," *National Public Radio*, September 1, 2010, http://www.npr.org/2010/09/01/129578263/at-war-s-end-u-s-ship-rescued-south-vietnam-s-navy.
8. "Fort Chaffee Maneuver Training Center," *Wikipedia*, https://en.wikipedia.org/wiki/Fort_Chaffee_Maneuver_ Training_Center.
9. "Vietnamese Boat People," *Wikipedia*, https://en.wikipedia.org/wiki/Vietnamese_boat_people.

10. "Richard J. Barohn, M.D.," University of Kansas Medical Center, http://www.kumc.edu/school-of-medicine/neurology/faculty/richard-j-barohn-md.html.

11. Nelson Allen, "Christmas to Be Extra Special for Teen Who Never Lost Hope," *San Antonio Express-News*, December 22, 1989.

12. "Datapoint," *Wikipedia*, https://en.wikipedia.org/wiki/Datapoint.

13. Ibid.

14. Ibid.

15. Ibid.

16. Ibid.

17. Ibid.

18. Stephen Solarz, "Our Responsibility to Refugees from Vietnam, Laos, and Cambodia," *The Bridge*, International Refugee Advocacy Center, June 1988.

19. Ibid.

20. Ibid.

21. Ibid.

22. Thu-Huong Ha, "Forty-One Years Ago, the US Took a Big Gamble on Vietnamese Refugees," *Quartz*, April 30, 2016.

23. Lomi Kriel, "Vietnamese Refugees Broaden City's Culture," Chron.com, September 10, 2016.

ABOUT THE AUTHORS

THUHANG TRAN was born in Saigon and developed polio as a toddler. When Saigon fell in 1975, her father narrowly escaped to the United States and left his family behind. Later, the family was told that he had been killed in a helicopter crash. It took almost fifteen years for Thuhang's family to be reunited. When Thuhang immigrated to America, she had surgery and intense physical therapy that enabled her to stand upright after crawling and squatting on the floor for seventeen years. She went on to start her new life by learning English, graduating from college, and working at several Fortune 500 companies in information technology. Several years ago, she focused her energy on helping orphaned and disabled children in Vietnam. Her future goals include creating a nonprofit organization to help disabled children in Vietnam.

SHARON ORLOPP is an expert on everyday inclusion. As the global chief diversity officer and senior vice president of human resources for Walmart, she created unique experiential immersion trips to teach others about different cultures. As an author, editor, and speaker, she is passionate about building a world where every person is valued and included. Sharon believes in the transformative power of personal stories to touch the heart, which in turn changes behaviors.

Map of Vietnam War Theater
Courtesy of Encyclopædia Britannica, Inc.

Dad with me on his lap, my sister, Linh Phuong,
and my brother, Quang Phuong.

Dad at the Da Nang airport control tower. This photo
was in his valise with his personal belongings.

Mom, Grandma, Quang Phuong, and Linh Phuong.

Posing during my preteen years.

This is one of the family photos I secretly hid in a tin can.

We sent Dad this photo in 1980 when we heard that he was alive. Quang Phuong is wearing Dad's military hat.

Wearing shirts for Tet celebration that my sister made from fabric Dad sent us. Left to right: Linh Phuong, me (leaning on table and with help from my sister), Mom, and Quang Phuong.

Dad standing in front of his house in San Antonio. This is the photo he provided us when we heard that he was alive.

Quang Phuong and Ngoc Dung's wedding.
Left to right: Aunt Kim, Mom, Ngoc Dung, Quang Phuong,
Grandpa Ong Noi, Uncle Truc, Uncle Dinh.

One of the many goodbye parties before we left
Vietnam to be reunited with Dad. Mom is wearing the *ao dai*,
a Vietnamese traditional outfit, and I am sitting in the middle.

Our first Christmas in San Antonio.
Left to right: Lynn, Mom, me, and Peter.

Graduation day at
the University of Texas
at San Antonio.

Standing upright after surgery.

Spending time with my nieces and nephews.
Front row: Sonny, Theresa, me. Back row: Jackie, Richie, Tony.

Dad and me with his grandkids.
Left to right: Sonny, Richie, Dad, Tony, me, and Theresa.

Dad was featured in
his company's newsletter
about the work he had
done at Datapoint.

Celebrating Dad's
seventy-second birthday.
I'm grateful for everything
he has taught me about
hope, determination, and
personal reinvention.